The 15 Success Traits of Pro Bloggers

JONATHAN MILLIGAN

D1403408

JONATHAN MILLIGAN

YOUR TWO FREE GIFTS

As a way of saying thanks for your purchase, we're offering two free gifts that are exclusive to our book and blog readers.

First up is the one-page roadmap that outlines the entire book. This is a beautiful color PDF you can print off and hang next to you as you build your online blogging business. It reinforces the 15 success traits you are about to learn in this book.

Next is a free video training series I have created for you. If you want to dive deeper into what it takes to go *from a passionate idea to a profitable online business*, then you'll want to grab this free video training series!

To get your free gifts, go to:

BloggingYourPassion.com/book

CONTENTS

THE BLOGGING SUCCESS PYRAMID

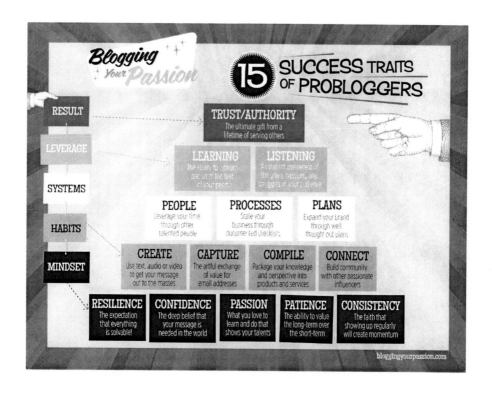

INTRODUCTION

You can do this. You just need a proven roadmap to follow.

There was a time in the not-too-distant past when I struggled with blogging. At times I felt that, no matter what I did, I just couldn't grow my blog traffic to the next level. With so many things to do, I was confused about where I should spend my time. There was so much advice online—some good, mostly bad. I never felt more alive than when I was blogging, but I wondered if anyone was even really listening.

Then there came the desire to earn money with my blog. How was I going to do that and not feel like a crooked salesman? I didn't feel comfortable thrusting myself into the limelight as the hero who has his act together and knows all the answers.

I also doubted myself as well. The fear of not being good enough crept in, took residence, and whispered to me that I just didn't have what it takes to be a success. Why does this seem so much easier for everyone else? People I knew seemed to be growing at a faster rate than I was. What was wrong with me?

Have you been there?

Maybe that is how you feel in this moment. You come fully alive when you think about blogging and sharing your passion with the world—only to abandon the dream due to your own negative thoughts and self-sabotage.

Can I encourage you for a moment?

Let the words of Hal Elrod in his book The Miracle Morning sink deep into your soul: "You are just as worthy, deserving, and capable of creating and sustaining extraordinary health, wealth, happiness, love, and success in your life, as any other person on earth."

So, I went on a journey.

I decided that in order to be successful as a Pro Blogger, I needed to adopt the mindset, habits, and systems of full-time bloggers. If I could somehow deconstruct what all the full-time bloggers were doing and find a pattern, I would have a roadmap to follow. I've spent the last few years interviewing, discussing, interacting and learning from all the best full-time bloggers out there. What I have found is that they all have fifteen success traits in common. I've distilled all of my research, interviews and life experience into the pages of this book.

This book is not a bunch of random ideas that work today but not tomorrow. It's a roadmap that will be just as relevant ten years from now. It's not about the latest tools and software. Tools come and go, but principles are always true. I've done the research of analyzing what the best bloggers in the world do, where they spend their time, and what matters most to them in building their business.

This book is for bloggers, podcasters, coaches, platform builders, and online entrepreneurs. If you desire to build an online business, this book is for you. Here are a few of the things you'll learn in the pages ahead:

- An easy-to-follow roadmap that outlines the entire book
- A proven pathway that's been approved by other full-time bloggers
- Insights based on my own six-year blogging journey
- Evergreen advice that highlights proven principles

If you're tired of all the confusing advice out there, it's time to settle into a process you can trust.

You can do this. You just need a proven roadmap to follow. Turn the page for the roadmap.

Chapter One

Why Blogging?

Before we jump into the roadmap and the success traits, it's important to note why blogging is so vital to building your online business and platform. While some say blogging is dead, I beg to differ. In fact, I think you'll be convinced that blogging is alive and well after reading this list of the amazing benefits of blogging.

27 Amazing Benefits Of Blogging

1. Blogging offers you the ability to pursue your passion. I can think of no other vehicle than blogging that allows anyone anywhere to influence anyone anywhere. The topics are endless and the world is just outside the "publish" button.

2. Blogging builds a platform for you. Whether you are a speaker, author, leader of an organization or stay-at-home mom, blogging gives you the opportunity to build a platform that enables you to indulge your expertise and passion.

3. Blogging is a low-cost way to build a business. A $10 domain name and a $3-a-month hosting package puts you in business. Blogging is the ultimate low-cost startup.

4. Blogging refines your writing skills. Blogging allows you to learn on the go. With each published blog post, you get that much better. The more you write, the better you become over time.

5. Blogging offers you the potential to connect with other influencers. Another fantastic benefit of blogging is the amazing relationships that you can develop. You get to connect with other influencers in the blogosphere. There is nothing more rewarding than connecting with other bloggers who share your passion.

6. Blogging increases your knowledge base. I have often said that the best bloggers are learners at heart. They love to learn and then share what they have learned with the world.

7. Blogging engages people in a conversation. I love the comment section of a blog. A blog post is just a conversation starter. Over the years, I have been both encouraged and challenged by the comments on my blog. Like iron sharpens iron, comments from others sharpen my thinking.

8. Blogging stretches you beyond your comfort zone. You have to be willing to put yourself out there a bit. Blogging opens you up and exposes your thoughts, ideas and opinions. Not everyone is going to agree with you, but that is okay too.

9. Blogging solves problems for people. There is nothing like receiving a comment about how something you wrote solved a problem for someone. The only thing to top that is receiving a comment about how something you wrote *two years ago* helped somebody *today*. Talk about maximizing your influence!

10. Blogging is a great place to test ideas. I have had good ideas and bad ideas over the years. When you blog, you offer the opportunity to see if others feel the same way you do. Maybe your crazy idea is not so crazy after all!

11. Blogging provides social proof for any adventure. Many book publishers today are looking at your blog to see how many real followers you have (Facebook, Twitter, mailing lists, etc.). Building social proof on your site opens up a whole new world of possibilities for you. Not to mention that your blog provides a central hub for all your social media efforts.

12. Blogging has a far-reaching effect. I totally missed the potential reach aspect of a blog when I started. The weekend I launched my first product, I had two people from Australia purchase it. That weekend changed my thinking from that day forward. Today, it is not unusual for me to have a coaching call with someone on the East Coast and the West Coast in the same day.

13. Blogging is sustainable over the long run. It is hard for me to imagine a world where blogging does not have some type of impact. It may change a bit over the years, but the principles will never change. There will always be people seeking information.

14. Blogging makes you a better thought leader. One of the absolute joys of writing for me is seeing how my thoughts develop. Blogging can stretch your thinking in a way that no other medium can.

15. Blogging makes you a better communicator. Each article I write has a purpose to it. There is a "big idea" and a logical outline to follow. Every point supports that big idea in a specific way. Each article is like crafting a sermon or developing a keynote speech. Once you are offered a speaking opportunity, you'll have plenty of pre-crafted speech outlines ready to go!

16. Blogging increases your ability to lead. If you are a leader of an organization, you need a blog. Period. Blogging offers you the ability to influence, increase your leadership and propel your vision. Blogging allows you to get up close and personal with everyone in your organization. They know what is on your mind and in your heart.

17. Blogging makes you a better listener. Readers of my blog have influenced my thinking over the years. I love to hear other perspectives.

18. Blogging positions you as an expert. I still remember the day that a reporter from Monster.com called me requesting an interview. After only one year of blogging about career-related topics, this was a real highlight for me. Put your knowledge and experience out there and over time you will establish yourself as an expert in your niche.

19. Blogging gives you a voice. We all want our lives to matter. Blogging gives you a voice in this world. What you say can make an impact on someone else. You have a message. Your message is needed in the world.

20. Blogging assists you in building a tribe of followers. Whether it is building a mailing list or creating products that others love, blogging gives you the ability to create a band of followers— people who join you in your journey and enjoy the same passions.

21. Blogging is a great personal branding tool. Blogging can increase your personal brand like nothing else. It displays your knowledge and shows the world what you are all about.

22. Blogging can assist you in publishing a book. If you desire to be an author, blogging can be a great avenue toward reaching your dream. Many successful authors started with blogging. Through a blog, you can create the content for your book and build a following who will purchase your book.

23. Blogging can assist you in getting new job offers. I have heard many stories about bloggers who were offered their dream job because of their blog. A blog becomes your résumé.

24. Blogging allows you to promote other bloggers and their messages. Another amazing benefit to blogging is having the ability to promote worthy causes, highlight talented authors, and build rising bloggers.

25. Blogging offers you the opportunity to be creative. There is nothing more creative than creating your own products. To see something go from just an idea to a finished product that helps others is incredibly humbling. Where else are you able to test out your creativity and earn income?

26. Blogging allows your thoughts and ideas to influence others 24/7. One of the things that I love most about blogging is that my doors are always open. I can influence someone with the words I write at 3:00 a.m. when I am asleep. I can spend the day with my family at the beach and my influence, ideas, and thoughts are still influencing others.

27. Blogging can earn you an income. I left this until last on the list because the longer I do this, the more I see it as the byproduct of everything listed above. Don't get me wrong; I love the fact that I can earn a living through blogging. But if you chase the income first, you will be left wanting. Instead, focus on providing tremendous value, building traffic, and making a difference. Then, making money with a blog becomes easier.

Convinced that blogging is an amazing tool for building your business? Now, let's open up the roadmap.

Chapter Two

The Blogging Success Pyramid

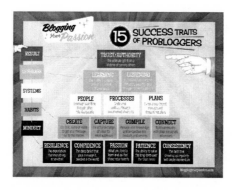

As early as 2011, I began a quest. My quest was to create a clear, concise roadmap anyone could follow to become a full-time blogger. I was tired of seeing and hearing all of the hype about getting rich with online businesses. There was no shortage of pictures of so-called "gurus" leaning against their Lamborghinis with the mansion in the backdrop.

I'm not even interested in buying a Lamborghini.

If you are like me, you just want to do what you love, make a difference in the lives of others, control your own schedule and work from home. Is that too much to ask? Was it really that farfetched of an idea? As you will see in the pages ahead, it's more possible today than ever before to live the life of your dreams. More and more people are trading the cubicle for the portable office and the suit and tie for the T-shirt and jeans. Today you can create a portable, lifestyle business that over time can become something great. It might not happen overnight, but it is definitely possible if you have a roadmap.

The Blogging Success Pyramid

I've had the fortunate opportunity to personally get to know many full-time bloggers over the past few years. I've studied their craft and observed where they spend their time. I've asked detailed questions to learn more about how they focus, what they avoid, and what they value. I've worked hard to synthesize everything I've learned into fifteen success traits you can incorporate into your online business.

Since this has been a three-year project in the making, I've changed, tweaked, and adjusted this framework until I was able to get it just right. You're seeing the result of three years of work and research as you read the pages ahead. I've even incorporated the lessons I've learned into my own online business over time. These principles work, if you work them. I'm living proof. I've successfully built the bridge from my day job to my dream job.

If you want to print off the Blogging Success Pyramid, I've made one available to you as a thank you for grabbing a copy of this book. Just go to: BloggingYourPassion.com/book.

There's No Need to Take a Leap

What I love about the success traits you are about to learn is all of these can be built in the margins of your life. Your online business can be your "side hustle" while you still have a day job. Will it be easy? No. Will it be worth it? Yes. Will you have to carve out extra time to build your online business? Yes. But it can be done.

Here are a few reasons a blogging business can be the perfect side hustle:

- Your blog is open 24/7 even when you are doing something else
- You can earn income on your blog while you are doing something else
- You can respond to e-mail and customers on your own time

The bottom line is that a blogging business allows you to build a bridge to your dream job so no leap is required or necessary.

The 4 Main Tiers of the Blogging Success Pyramid

I've divided the fifteen success traits into four main tiers. Each tier of the success pyramid builds upon the next. The bottom tier is the solid foundation that all Pro Bloggers have built in order to be successful. Let's take a brief look at each of the four tiers.

The Mindset of Pro Bloggers *(Chapters 3-8)*

What often separates the successful from the unsuccessful is their mindset. Pro Bloggers think differently. In fact, if any of them were to start over from scratch, they would reach success much faster the second time around. Why is that? Is it their talent? Is it some secret traffic loophole they are hiding from the rest of us? Nope. They have the right mindset. As you will learn in the pages ahead, your actions follow your thoughts. Change your thoughts—change your actions.

This bottom tier is called "the inner game of blogging." I gave it that name because there is a game going on inside your head. Steven Pressfield aptly called it *resistance*. The inner game going on between your own two ears is what's keeping you from fully going for it. Pro Bloggers understand and value the importance of resilience, confidence, passion, patience, and consistency.

The Habits of Pro Bloggers *(Chapters 9-13)*

Once we get the right mindset, we need to know where to best spend our time. If you haven't figured it out already, there are a million ways you can spend your time trying to build your online business. Every few months there is a new social media channel that everyone is telling us we have to be on. Every month there are new tools that are supposed to make our lives easier. Don't get me wrong—I'm all for using tools when it makes sense. But what I have found is that new tools can conveniently become a way to procrastinate and avoid the real work.

Pro Bloggers are relentless about how they spend their time. Many of them will not check e-mail or social media until their most important tasks are done for the day. They work on "event" time and not "clock" time. This is an important distinction to make if you are an employee who wants to work for yourself one day. *Event time* means *my work is done for the day when I get my most important work done. Clock time* means *I have to sit here until five o'clock this afternoon so I might as well pace myself.*

In the pages ahead, you'll learn about the four keystone habits all full-time bloggers have. Knowing and understanding what these four habits are will help you to say no to everything else. If you were to look at my weekly calendar, you'd find that these four habits consume 90-95% of my work schedule. They are that important. I'll even share with you how a typical workday looks in the life of a full-time blogger.

The Systems of Pro Bloggers *(Chapters 14-17)*

Once you've adopted the right mindset and mastered the keystone habits, how do you take things to the next level? After all, there is only so much of you to go around. The answer is in systems. All successful bloggers place high value on people, processes and plans in order to get to the next level. They instinctively know that they are not an expert at everything. They are better off focusing on the few areas where they shine. They document their processes so other people can help them grow their business. Pro Bloggers also place high priority on plans. You'll learn the three main plans they use to grow their businesses.

Reaching this level in your blogging business doesn't happen overnight. It is a process. It isn't something you *go* into—but *grow* into. Getting better organized and creating systems that foster growth is what all of the really successful bloggers do. Don't worry. We will show you how later in the book.

The Leverage of Pro Bloggers *(Chapters 18-20)*

Leverage is where the magic happens. This tier in the blogging pyramid is about more than just passive income and earning money while you sleep. The type of leverage you'll learn about in the chapters ahead is much more powerful. It's the kind of leverage that not only helps you get to the top, but stay on top for years to come.

It might surprise you as to what these two types of leverage are. You may have never thought of these as leverage points, but you'll soon discover why they hold so much power. This type of leverage helps you to stay relevant. In a world in which things change on a daily basis, this is vital to the longevity of your business.

Now that you have a better idea as to the framework of the pyramid, it's time to get started. Let's take a closer look at the bottom tier of the pyramid—*the inner game of blogging.*

Chapter Three

"Once your mindset changes, everything on the outside
will change along with it."
~Steve Maraboli

The Inner Game of Blogging

I call the bottom tier of the blogging success pyramid the *"inner game of blogging."* It's something not talked about in most blogging courses today. The thoughts and questions happening in your head will ultimately determine your actions. If you tell yourself you're too old, too young, or not smart enough, you'll quit.

Have you ever said to yourself any of the following?

- I'm just too busy. I can't find time to blog.
- I'm technically challenged so I'll probably never be successful at any of this.
- Other bloggers in my niche are way better than I am anyhow.

It's a choice. It's your choice today. If you are an aspiring blogger, I have five things I want you to stop saying today. Don't worry—I'll tell you what to say instead.

Myth #1. "I'm just going to follow the money and I'll be rich."

While the "Make money online" hype seems to have calmed down a bit compared to ten years ago, it still exists today. One of the main reasons I chose to start BloggingYourPassion.com was my desire to be a realistic voice in an unrealistic market. Yes, you definitely can earn money from home as a blogger, but you won't get rich because of a software or a secret Google traffic loophole.

In the middle of 2010, I became distracted. I was beginning to make a nice monthly income from Google AdSense and decided I needed to explore it further. So, I "followed the money." I set up niche blog sites on niche topics solely because they were good AdSense earners. By the end of the year, I sold the domains and pulled out of that strategy. Why? I wasn't passionate about the topics and I wasn't teaching or serving anyone with any value. Don't follow the money.

Answer: Passion—What you love to learn and do that shows your talents.

You're probably thinking: "Passion won't put food on my table." I agree. Later in this book, I'll show you how to build a business model around your passion. We live in an amazing time. You can work from your home, share your passion through teaching and serving others, and earn enough income to provide for your family.

My first blog was a career-coaching blog. When I started out, I knew of only three ways to earn money with my blog: career coaching, résumé writing, and advertising with Google AdSense. After 24 months of blogging, I had discovered and built 12 income buckets for my blog. I'm going to teach you how to do the same with your passion.

Myth #2. "I don't have what it takes."

Competition will often stop you in your tracks. The answer is to stop seeing others as competition. See them instead as people who share the same passion as you. Sure, they may be more talented than you in certain areas, but that doesn't negate your unique gift. Don't try to compare their success today with your humble beginnings. Here's a secret: *All of us have doubts as to whether or not we have what it takes.* Successful people acknowledge the doubts and decide to press forward anyways.

Answer: Confidence—The deep belief that your message is needed in the world.

Do you believe that your message can change lives? Whether you blog about personal finances, parenting, organic gardening, politics, or spiritual issues, you need to step forward with confidence that your message is needed in the world. If what you have to say can change someone's day, then it's your responsibility to say it, write it or record it.

Myth #3. "If this works, I'll be an instant success."

There is nothing wrong with being optimistic about a new blog, service, product, or book you are about to launch. The problem is our belief that we only need just one thing (insert name of your book, product, or service) in order to be successful. Many of us don't give our idea enough time to succeed because we started with unrealistic expectations. We sabotage our own success because we want to see the home run and we don't value the singles and the doubles. As Michael Hyatt explains it: "*Success is more like a bunch of singles and doubles.*"

Answer: Patience—The ability to value the long term over the short term.

I want you to adopt a different mindset instead. Embrace the "brick-by-brick" philosophy. Choose to see your next blog post, product, service, podcast or video as a brick you are laying for an amazing foundation you are building. Choose to value the long term over the short term. Luck happens to those who've been preparing backstage for a long time. We often admire people who appear to be successful fast. What we don't see is the years of hard work and preparation that took place when no one was watching.

Myth #4. "I don't know how to do this. I'm too technically challenged."

Pardon the French but technology sucks for all of us. Seriously. Earlier this year I did a joint webinar with a few other blogger friends. We all promoted it via our e-mail lists and created quite a buzz. My one responsibility was setting up the Google Hangout and embedding it onto a page. Easy, right? I've done it hundreds of times. This time, though, was a disaster. I felt like it was all my fault—because it was. I had wasted everyone's time. We only had thirty-two live viewers once I figured out what went wrong.

Answer: Resilience—The expectation that everything is solvable.

Technology challenges happen to all of us. It's just the way it is. Even when you reach the level of success you were hoping for, you'll still meet technology challenges. The difference is successful people believe that *everything is solvable*. If you want a mantra to hang by your computer, then borrow the one Marie Forleo taught me, which I repeat often: "*Everything is figureoutable.*" Don't let technology challenges stop you.

Myth #5. "I'm too busy. I just don't have enough time."

This is the biggest myth, and the one I hear the most. I get it. I know we are all busy. But let me ask you a question. I want you to think of any successful blogger you know and answer this question: "Were they less busy than I am when they were starting out?" Here is the truth: We all have the same amount of time each day. What we choose to do with our time tells us what's most important to us. Besides, quality time is more important than quantity of time.

Answer: Consistency—The faith that showing up regularly will create momentum.

Choose instead to be consistent. From your consistency you will gain momentum. When a blogger tells me they are too busy to blog, I encourage them to back down on the *frequency* at which they blog and be more *consistent* instead. Maybe for you it is better to select every Tuesday as the day you will publish a blog post. Pick a day and be consistent no matter what. Consistency is what breeds momentum.

I have found that finding time is not the issue for most aspiring bloggers. It's more of a focus issue: "When there's so much to do, where do I spend my time wisely?" I'm going to teach you the four keystone habits that every successful blogger makes a priority every single week. The real answer is being consistent in these four areas.

Over the next few chapters, we will be taking a deep dive into each of these mindsets. It is critically important you develop the mindset of a Pro Blogger if you are to have any hope of success. Your thoughts will determine your actions. Bad thinking results in inaction. Right thinking leads to right actions and good results.

Chapter Four

"Don't ask yourself what the world needs; ask yourself what makes you come alive. And then go and do that. Because what the world needs is people who have come alive." ~Howard Thurman

Success Trait #1

PASSION

What you love to learn and do that shows your talents

In the eighteenth century, being an immigrant of the United States was no easy road. Being an immigrant who was also a deaf-mute child with physical disabilities was even harder. When Andrew Clemens was only five years old he contracted a "brain fever," which we now know as encephalitis. Unfortunately, this severe fever left Andrew deaf in both ears.

One day while growing up in Iowa, Andrew became fascinated by the various colors of sandstones in the cliffs. He began placing layers of this sand into bottles just for fun. As people saw this beautiful artwork, they began to pay Andrew to create more. Eventually, this became his full-time job. Andrew Clemens had invented a new art form: *sand art*.

When I think of this story it reminds me of a core truth I believe to be true: *You have a gift. Your gift is needed in the world.* Thomas Edison said, "If we did all the things we are capable of doing, we would literally astound ourselves." When is the last time you surprised yourself?

You Have a Gift

I'm often surprised at how many people don't believe they have a unique gift. We often discount our own gift. We're too close to see it to even value it. We mistakenly believe that since something comes easy to us, it must be easy for everyone. Not true. What would your life be like if you decided to lean into your own unique gift? Proverbs 18:16 states, "A man's gift makes room for him and brings him before great men."

When you lean into your gift, you are never more in sync with the God who created you. Leo Buscaglia said it best when he said, "Your talent is God's gift to you. What you do with it is your gift back to God."

Myth #1: "I'm just going to follow the money and I'll be rich."

For way too long the wrong message has been told about building an online business. What makes us believe that building an online business is any different from building a traditional business? If anything, it's become more crowded online. The good news is you don't need many true fans to truly build a rewarding online business.

Still, we focus our attention on the rare exceptions. We see those who seem to have built their riches overnight and think the same should happen for us. Instead of looking for areas of passion where we can teach and serve others, we chase money instead. We choose topics based on the wealth they can potentially provide for us instead of the things for which we have real abiding passion.

Money Will Never Fill Your Purpose Bucket

If you imagine that I've never fallen for this trap, let me set you straight. We are all susceptible to chasing after money. There's nothing wrong with money—but money alone won't fill your purpose bucket.

Back in 2010, I was beginning to earn some decent money blogging but not enough yet to leave my day job. One of my streams of income was Google AdSense. AdSense is a program that allows you to earn money anytime a visitor clicks on the ads on your site. As my monthly AdSense checks began to rise to almost $1000+ a month, I began to explore ways to earn more of it.

I came across a forum where AdSense earners were making thousands and tens of thousands of dollars each month with AdSense. They were earning this money by creating "niche blogs" on very narrow topics such as solar pool covers, black mold removal, and bad credit repair. Being fascinated by this income model, I dove head in. While still keeping my main blogs, I wanted to create 30+ niche blogs. After a few months, I had around 15 sites up with AdSense as my income strategy. After three more months, I came to the realization that I just wasn't fulfilled in what I was doing.

I had zero passion to research and write about solar pool covers all day. I was earning more income, but was not satisfied. I couldn't connect the dots on how I was making a difference. If anything I was publishing mediocre content that may have been more confusing to the end consumer. I quickly made a pivot and sold all of my niche sites. That's the day I returned to my passions. It's also the main reason I chose my domain name: BloggingYourPassion.com. I believe the world is better served when you and I teach and share our passions.

Why in the End Your Passion Really Isn't About You

Before you begin to think that chasing your gifts and passions is all about you, let me make a definitive point. In the end, your passion really isn't even about you. The people you teach and serve through your passions are the real heroes. You are just the guide, who offers a roadmap that others can follow. Your roadmap or framework, as we will learn later, helps to solve a specific problem. As long as you see yourself as the hero, you'll struggle at building a successful blog. All Pro Bloggers know and understand this secret. They place their focus on speaking the dialogue that's going on in the hearts and minds of their audience. If you really would like to dive deep into this concept of Story Branding, I'd encourage you to take a look at the work Don Miller is providing at StoryBrand.com.

Your platform, regardless of how big or small, is really about stewarding your gift, and serving as many people as possible. I love the words of Rabbi Daniel Lapin, who says, *"Work is not about doing what you want to do; work is about serving others."*

If You're Not Passionate About Your Message, Don't Start a Blog

It's vitally important that the topic or umbrella theme of your blog be something you are personally passionate about. When you are not passionate about your message:

1. You start with the wrong motives. There is certainly nothing wrong with earning money from a blog. In fact, in many ways you serve your audience better by offering products for sale. If you're not passionate about your message, your quality will always suffer. When I was trying to grow "niche" blogs, I became so bored with writing on topics I had no interest in that I began paying other people to write them. I'm embarrassed to say that I published low-quality articles because I just wasn't interested in value. I was only interested in production.

2. You have no deep well to draw from. Another reason you need to be passionate about your message is so you can be a leading learner. A leading learner never runs out of things to talk about because they have a natural drive to learn more about that topic. Do you have a deep well to draw from? You should pursue a message that you don't see yourself becoming weary of anytime soon.

3. You won't survive the pre-profit stage of your blog. We will talk more about this a bit later, but regardless of what your blog is about, there will be a pre-profit stage; i.e., a length of time (usually longer than we want) during which we consistently share our message without much attention or income. The only thing that is going to get you through this time is if you are truly passionate about your message.

4. You are better off with a "worldview" than a "niche." I thank Jeff Goins for building this perspective into my life. It's hard to get passionate about a niche, but it is easy to get passionate about a worldview. Having a worldview allows you to be you. Following after a niche often makes you become something you don't really want to be. A worldview allows you to share your opinion, vision, and unique perspective, which will cause others to either passionately connect or politely disagree. It's hard to share a worldview and not be passionate to some degree.

There are many experts who say that "following your passion" is a bad idea. I believe differently. If Gary Vaynerchuk built his business talking about wine, you can build a business on your passion. Of course it goes without saying that your blog has to be useful and you need to provide solutions, but it can be done.

What You Love to Learn and Do That Shows Your Talent
What then should we choose to build our blog and online business around? The answer is *your passion*. Your #1 job as a blogger is to teach and serve others. You'll need to give much more than you take if you are going to be a success. If you don't come from a place of passion, you'll never be able to authentically teach and serve others.

4 Ways to Select the Right Passion to Pursue as a Blog

I can hear what you might be thinking at this point: "How do I discover my passion?" For a few of us, the answer is pretty obvious, but for others it feels like a mystery. After working with thousands of passion seekers, let me provide you with some clues that might help.

1. You'll find your passion in what you already love to learn about. Our true passions are often hidden in the areas we gravitate toward in everyday life. They are often so obvious to us that we just don't notice them right away. For example:

- When at the bookstore, which sections do you gravitate toward?

- When locked into a conversation, which topics do you gravitate toward?
- When watching videos online, which topics do you most want to learn?

Identifying the topics we naturally move toward is a great indicator as to our "no end path." Jonathan Mead uses the term "no end path" to describe the topics you love to learn about that will never grow old to you. Chances are, ten years from now you'll still have an interest in that topic. That's your *passion*.

2. You'll find your passion in what you already love to do that shows your talents. Just having passion for a topic is only one part of the equation. You'll also need to choose a passion that is helpful and useful to others. What is it that you naturally do well? What is it that causes others to stand up and take notice? If you are not sure, don't be afraid to ask three to four people who know you best. Ask them to share three words that best describe you. Ask them what they believe makes you unique. Ask them what strengths they see in you.

3. You'll find your passion in your deep struggles and what you've already been through in life. Another great area to explore is your past struggles. Chances are if you've been through a deep struggle in life, you have some passion behind how you came out of that struggle. You have a story to tell. You have a unique perspective that others want to hear. You have solutions that others will gladly pay you for. Many newbie bloggers mistakenly think that they must come from a place of mastery and authority to even be respected. Pro Bloggers understand that they connect better with their audience when their messes become their message.

4. You'll find passion in the area that you're willing to live and breathe for the next five years. A good litmus test as to whether or not you have chosen the right passion to pursue as a blog would be to answer this question: "*Am I willing to live and breathe this for the next five years?*" Success is possible but often doesn't happen overnight. You'll need to be willing to live and breathe your passion for awhile before you reach your ultimate destination of trust and authority. Never forget that every Pro Blogger you admire today once blogged in entire obscurity. Selecting the right passion and having the right mindset will set you apart from everyone else.

A Word for the Multi-Passionate Blogger

What do you do if you have multiple passions? Many of us would classify ourselves as multi-passionate. I know I have certainly struggled in the past with the following questions:

- Which of my many passions is the best choice for starting a blog?
- Out of all my passions, which one resonates best with others?

- What if the passion I want to blog about has too much competition already?

Have you ever wrestled with any of those questions? Maybe you feel similar to an e-mail I received from a fellow blogging student:

"I've been going through your Blogging 101 course, and I can't decide what topic to try. I have a few ideas so far: health, fitness, goals and fashion. Can you help me narrow it down? I've gone through the video that helps me with that, but I still can't decide. Every time I decide on one, I end up wanting the other one as well."

Here was my answer back:

"I completely understand where you are coming from. Having multiple passions is tough. One idea is to combine some of your passions into one blog. NerdFitness.com is a great example. He talks about video games and fitness on the same blog. You can also go with a personal branding blog and use your own name. Your name is something that will never change (unless you are a single female). This way you can share your many passions under one blog. Another example is theArtrofNonConformity.com. Chris has an umbrella theme of freedom/living different and yet he talks about travel, working while traveling, and living different all on one blog. See if there is an 'overarching theme' to your various passions."

If you need a logical approach to selecting the right passion for your blog, then allow me to introduce you to the Idea Filter Worksheet. This is a worksheet that I introduced to my Teach Your Passion students. It is designed to help you to logically choose which idea is the best one to turn into an online course. I believe the same questions can work for analyzing our passions as well. Choose one passion at a time, then score yourself on a scale of one to ten for each of the following questions.

- How much do I enjoy learning about this topic?
- How passionate am I about this topic/worldview?
- What's my level of experience or skill with this?
- Am I able to solve problems or satisfy desires of other people with this topic or worldview?
- Are other people already earning income with this topic or worldview? (If yes, this is a positive sign, not a negative one.)

After you walk your many passions through these questions, total up your score. How did you do? Which of your passions had the highest score? Did one or two passions rise to the top? If one was a clear winner, go with that one. If you still have two or three with similar scores, select an umbrella theme that allows you to pursue all of them under one blog.

Choosing the Right Domain Name for Your Blog

Once you've selected your passion, umbrella theme or worldview for your blog, it's time to select the right domain name.

- **Select a memorable name.** You'll want to have a domain name that is easy to remember. Be sure that it is not too long or too confusing. You'll want to have top-of-the-mind awareness to make it easier for others to share your blog.

- **Go with a .com if at all possible.** You can grow a nice blog without a .com extension but it's where I'd recommend you start. If the .com of your desired domain name is taken, then .org is your next best bet, followed by .net.

- **Do not use dashes in your domain name.** I know of some bloggers who wanted a name so badly that they chose to put a dash in the domain name. I strongly urge you to avoid dashes if at all possible. As you become more popular, others referring to your blog will more than likely not add the dash resulting in a dead link and no referral traffic for you. You do not want that headache.

- **Be aware of how your domain name reads with the words smushed together.** Before you buy that domain name you want, run it by a few people first. Sometimes, when we have three or four words in our domain name, they can appear as different words when smushed together. An example would be the classic domain names speedofart.com and therapist.com. It should go without saying, but if you look close enough you can find two alternative meanings with these words smushed together.

Once you have chosen the right passion and selected the correct domain name, it's time to move on to our next critical mindset— *confidence*.

Chapter Five

"There is not passion to be found playing small—in settling for a life that is less than the one you are capable of living." ~*Nelson Mandela*

Success Trait #2

CONFIDENCE

The deep belief that your message is needed in the world

Are you hesitant about fully going for it? There was once a famous trapeze artist who was teaching his students the art of being a star performer on the trapeze bar. One particular student was having a difficult time fully going for it and was often filled with fear. "I can't do it! I can't do it!" the student gasped. The instructor put his hand on the student's shoulder and said, "Son, you can do it, and I will tell you how." He then made a statement I will never forget:

"Throw your heart over the bar and the rest will follow."

You know what my #1 problem was for a long time? I wasn't throwing my heart over the bar. I would dabble here and dabble a little bit there.

- I wanted results without the work.

- I wanted proof of a harvest without any serious planting.

- I wanted to know with absolute certainty that something was going to work before I invested any thought in it.

- I wanted to receive well beyond what I was willing to give.

Do any of those describe you today? If so, I want to help you take a different path. I want to encourage you to throw your heart over the bar. How would your situation be different a year from now if you chose to just *fully go for it?*

Myth #2: "I Don't Have What it Takes."

When I was just 22 years of age, I was thrust into a speaking engagement with over 600 church pastors in attendance. What made this challenge even more scary is each had a grading sheet in hand. Talk about pressure. My college degree was in Church Ministries and one of the required classes was Homiletics, which is the art of speaking or delivering messages to an audience. I was selected as one of the top three in my class, which meant I received the opportunity to be judged by over 600 pastors during the college graduation week festivities. Some reward, right?

I still remember some of the thoughts that raced through my mind:

- Who am I? I'm just a kid when it comes to this stuff.
- Do I really possess the ability to deliver a message that can be impactful to others?
- Is this something that God has even given me the ability to do?

To make it worse, right before I went on stage, a pastor tapped me on the shoulder and said, "Do you know who is sitting behind you? It's the pastor of one of the largest churches in the South. Just thought you should know."

Thanks—that just made it so much easier.

I did my thing the best I knew how. To my surprise, I was voted number one by the pastors in attendance that day. But that wasn't the biggest lesson I learned. When you get to the end of your life, you will treasure the moments when you decided to push past fear and try something new.

Overcoming the Fear of Not Being Good Enough

Have you ever faced the fear of not being good enough? Feelings of inadequacy and rejection can immobilize us and creep up in our lives without us even knowing it. The fear of not being good enough might be the very reason you are still sitting on the sidelines in life. No one wants to feel like they do not measure up. No one welcomes rejection and failure into their life.

I was reading a discussion forum recently and this very subject came up. A person was wanting to start a blog in a subject they were passionate about. However, when they viewed the competition, they began to seriously doubt whether they could pull it off. The fear of not being good enough began to creep in.

- I don't have everything figured out in my *own* life so how can I lead others?
- Maybe a more mature person is better suited for this; I am probably too young.
- What if I do this and it's a complete failure?

The fear of not being good enough begins to slowly take over.

A few years ago, my wife opened up to me about blogging. She had been secretly thinking about starting a blog. The theme of her blog was a great choice and something she was no doubt gifted in. Yet, her exact words to me were: *"I'm hesitant because I think other people could do it much better."*

The fear of not being good enough can be paralyzing.

I want to share with you some principles I have learned that have helped me to face the fear and do it anyways. If you find yourself sitting on the sidelines, my hope and prayer is you'll find strength in these principles.

1. The Principle of Leading from the Front

This principle has helped me in so many ways, especially when first starting out. Instead of focusing on what you lack, lead from what you *do* know. You only need to be a little bit ahead to add value in someone else's life. For example, if you are a blogger who only makes an average of $500 a month on your blog, there are plenty of people out there who want to learn from you. They would give anything to know what you know. You do not have to wait until you are "super successful" in order to begin assisting others. You just have to be a bit further ahead on the journey.

2. The Principle of You-niqueness

I am not talking about unique content, a unique domain name, or a unique blog theme. You can take confidence in just being *you*. You have been given unique talents, abilities, experience and knowledge. Other people can learn from you. Whenever I'm asked, "How do you stand out as a blogger when it's so crowded?" My answer to them is to stop copying others and be a more authentic you. There will never be another person who thinks, acts, and processes information exactly the way you do. Give the topic of "budgeting" to ten people and you will get ten different articles. Why is that? Because each of us possesses unique perspectives, experiences, personalities, and advice. People want to hear from you and not a textbook.

3. The Principle of Attractive Character

Can I help you out with something? You will never be an expert. I don't say that to be unkind. This fact should be a relief to you. We are all growing. We are all learning. None of us have arrived. I believe the best bloggers are "learners" at heart and not "writers." They share with others what they are learning on a regular basis. You do not have to write as an expert to gain a following. It's much more powerful when people connect with you as a person. JD Roth at Get Rich Slowly started writing about personal finance when he was in over his head. The blog Man vs Debt was started by Adam Baker who was under a ton of debt when he started his blog. Put yourself out there and let people connect with *you* the person.

4. The Principle of Continual Generosity

This is a principle I am trying to teach my kids on a regular basis. Life is not about how much you collect, but how much you give. Every day before they go off to school I tell them, "*Make it a great day for someone.*" I want them to know that the universe does not revolve around them. There is a great saying in Proverbs that says, "Some people are always greedy for more, but the godly love to give." It should be less about you and your wants and more about what you are giving. That takes the pressure off of rejection. Giving to others can be a powerful motivation for starting a blog. It was the main reason I started my first blog. I wanted to share everything I knew about the job search so that others could stumble upon it and be helped during the Great Recession.

Are you sitting on the sidelines in life? Has the fear of not being good enough paralyzed you? Work these principles into your life and step forward anyways. People are waiting to hear from you.

The Deep Belief That Your Message is Needed in the World

Confidence comes when you have a deep belief that your message is needed in the world. Most Pro Bloggers passionately understand this truth. They understand it so deeply that their message is more important than their personal popularity. In the book *Everyone Communicates, Few Connect*, author John Maxwell shares four questions which he suggests you ask yourself, to see whether you are passionate about your message:

1. Do I believe what I say?
2. Has it changed me?
3. Do I believe it will help others?
4. Have I seen it change others?

When I lack confidence, I ask myself those four questions. Immediately my mindset shifts from me onto my message. Be careful that your lack of confidence is not an underlying ego problem. When the ego is in charge, we value emotional comfort above all else. By placing confidence in the belief that our message has the power to improve lives, our mindset shifts to serving our audience well.

I know what you are thinking—I've heard it myself: "I have a message I'm passionate about, but there's too much competition already. There are already too many people trying to do the thing I want to do." What if that was a *good* thing? What if you saw that as social proof that people will pay you for it? The truth is, there will never be another "you." Just like your fingerprint is unique, you are unique. You bring a unique view, personality and perspective to all you do. Embrace that. Decide today to lean into your gift and make it useful for others.

- If you don't say it, it may never be said.
- If you don't write it, it may never be written.
- If you don't create it, it may never be created.

You have a message. Your message is needed in the world.

Chapter Six

"Through it all, I had some discouraging times when it seemed as though nothing was happening. But not only did I have the dream, the dream had me."

~Zig Ziglar

Success Trait #3

PATIENCE

The ability to value the long-term over the short-term

If it took 20 years for your dream to become a reality, would that be okay with you? Most of us would probably answer with an emphatic, "No!" But 20 years was the amount of time it took for Zig Ziglar's dream to come true. More than anything, Zig wanted to be a full-time speaker. For years, he would speak for free anywhere people would have him. What kept him going all those years? Well, in Zig's own words, *"The dream had me."*

It may not take 20 years for your dream to become a reality, but either way patience is required. Patience is a hard mindset to develop when we see so many examples of people who became wealthy quickly with their ideas.

Myth #3: "If this works, I'll be an instant success!"

Have you ever had that thought? It probably started with a late-night infomercial. We've all heard the hype of fast online riches. "Just send out an e-mail and rake in $24,000 in 24 hours," he tells you. To make it even more confusing, we see people who seem to have "gotten lucky" fairly quickly.

Since they did it, we can do it too. We start chasing the exceptions while ignoring the rules.

- The rules tells us it will take longer than we think—but we don't listen.
- The rules tell us we will have to work really hard for it—but we don't listen.
- The rules tell us success is more of a marathon than a sprint—but we don't listen.

Is it any wonder that most of us get discouraged so quickly? We throw our hands up and wonder what we are doing wrong. We stop working hard because, "What's the use anyways?" We lose hope.

The Instant Success Syndrome

Many online entrepreneurs have fallen prey to the Instant Success Syndrome. They try just hard enough to see whether they get more results than the effort they put in. If their expectations are not met, they either quit or paint other, more successful, people as liars. The Instant Success Syndrome has swallowed up many aspiring bloggers.

"Jonathan, I lost my job and I need to make this blogging thing work now in the next 30 days." I've heard several variations of that statement, more times that I can count. My advice back to them may seem harsh, but it is true: "Go get a job and build this blog on the side." Do I tell others that because I don't think you can build an online business quickly? No. However, why do we think that building an online business is any different from any other business?

What if I told you a simple mindset shift can change all of this for you?

The Ability to Value the Long Term over the Short Term

The "brick-by-brick" philosophy will save you lots of heartache. What if instead you told yourself, "It may take three years to build the online business of my dreams, but I'll be able to enjoy it for the next 20-30 years." What if you saw each task, project, or product as another brick you are laying into your foundation.

One of my favorite quotes of all time is from Peter Drucker who said, "We greatly overestimate what we can accomplish in one year and underestimate what we can accomplish in five years." This is true for all of us. There is nothing wrong with being optimistic and setting your vision high, but without patience for that vision, you'll quit.

Embracing the Pre-Profit Days of Blogging

Have you ever thought about the fact that every single full-time blogger once had a "pre-profit season" for their blog?

- They wrote blog posts without receiving a single blog comment.
- They participated on social media with very few followers.
- They nervously reached out to other, more successful, bloggers.
- They created products wondering if anyone was even interested in buying.

To value the long term means to embrace the pre-profit days of your blog. Once I discovered this truth, it allowed me to settle into the lengthy journey of sharing my message over a long period of time. You must value the journey more than the destination. You have to find fulfillment in the gap.

Finding Fulfillment in the Gap

Oftentimes, we think we won't be totally fulfilled or happy until we reach a certain destination. The truth is, those who accomplish their dreams have learned the value of finding fulfillment in the gap.

What is the Gap?

The gap is the space of time between where you are currently and where you ultimately want to be. In the world of blogging, it could be the gap between starting a blog and earning a full-time income from it. Most of us never think about enjoying the journey and being satisfied with where we currently are. If you have 500 unique monthly visitors to your blog, those who are just getting started would die to be where you are now—and yet you are unhappy. Don't get me wrong; a little bit of frustration can drive us to new heights. Still, we are more likely to quit if we don't find some fulfillment along the way.

How to Find Fulfillment in the Gap

1. Appreciate any step that moves you forward. There is no such thing as an overnight success in blogging. It just does not happen. Can it happen in a year or even two years? Yes! Success in blogging is often consistent, slow growth over time. However, when you expand your timeframe out, it is fast. What is a year or two of hard work if the result is a sustainable, legitimate online business? You will have to work hard for it, but it will be worth it.

While you are in the middle of all this hard work, you will not see or feel the immediate impact for awhile. We call it embracing the pre-profit time in the life of your blog. Yes, it will feel like you are working for free, but every single blog post you write and podcast you record will now be read and listened to for years to come.

What did you do this week in the life of your blog that you can sit back and smile at?

- Did you purchase a domain name for a new idea?
- Write several new blog posts in a week?
- Get your first comment on your blog?
- Make your first sale?
- Get your first AdSense click?

Whatever it is, take time to appreciate the everyday happenings of your blog. This will keep you moving forward.

2. Embrace new discoveries you find along the way. There is much to learn about blogging. The truth is, learning never stops; there is always something new you could implement in the life of your blog. What happens is we often beat ourselves up for doing something the wrong way for such a long time. Even worse, we are afraid to take action toward blogging, out of fear of not doing it right. After all, who wants to waste their time? This fear can immobilize us to stay right where we are. It is better to *fail forward.* Whenever I take action, as weak as it may be, new opportunities always open up as a result. What new discovery have you recently made that is going to make you better?

3. Have a real love for the journey. Here is an important principle to remember: *"It is the journey toward our goals that gives us purpose—not just reaching the destination."* If you truly love what you are doing, then it doesn't really feel like work. Sure, it takes effort and energy to do anything worthwhile, but if you love writing, find fulfillment in the actual writing and not just in whether or not you get 46 blog comments from it. One of my favorite quotes comes from Ursula K. Le Guin, who states, *"It is good to have an end to journey towards, but it is the journey that matters in the end."*

4. Focus on finding ways to add value instead. Is your motivation for a successful blog selfish? That is a big question, isn't it? Only you can answer this question honestly. If it is selfish, it comes across on your blog in many ways: the style in which you write; how you connect with others; and whether or not you see other bloggers in your niche as threats. Before you can really begin to make financial deposits from your blogging, you have to make emotional deposits in the lives of others. Add value anywhere and wherever you can.

Answer your e-mails when readers take the time to write you. Respond to blog comments if at all possible. Go out of your way, going above and beyond to invest and build up someone else. Your reputation is contagious. That counts whether it's good or bad.

Have you taken time to find fulfillment in the gap? Are you discouraged because you are not seeing success fast enough? Find ways to enjoy the journey. Besides, happy, positive people get more done. Decide today to settle in for a long yet fulfilling journey. This road you are on requires patience, but with this patience you're also going to need resilience.

Chapter Seven

"Success is not final, failure is not fatal:
it is the courage to continue that counts."
~*Winston Churchill*

Success Trait #4

RESILIENCE

The expectation that everything is solvable!

Have you ever been stuck in a potentially dangerous situation? I
am the oldest of three boys. When we were younger, we lived on
45-acre campground. The camp housed seven actual horses on
the property (some of which seemed wild at times). One fall
when I was about ten years old, my brothers and I decided to
venture over the fence to get a closer look at the horses. They
were just on the horizon down the hill so we strategized on how
we could get them to come closer. Not having any grain to shake
in the bucket (which usually caused them to run in our
direction), we decided to shake some rocks in the bucket instead.

Sure enough, all seven horses come galloping our way. When
they were about 50 yards away, I began to realize they were not
slowing down. I yelled, "*Run!*" I jumped over the fence and
made it to safety. Only one problem—my youngest brother was

stuck in the mud. The deep grooves from the horses and all of the rain caused his little shoes to stick deep in the mud. I quickly jumped back over the fence and pulled him right out of his shoes just in time.

Have you ever felt stuck? Have you ever felt hopeless at times? Life has its way of piling up on us. Whether it is problems with finances, school, work, or relationships, we often see no way out. When this frustration is attached to our dreams, it escalates. We lose hope of reaching our dreams because the journey is too hard and the road is too high.

Myth #4: "I don't know how to do this. I'm just too technically challenged."

Roadblocks are discouraging. Many aspiring bloggers have quit over technical challenges. *"I just don't know how to do this stuff"* becomes the mantra of the day. Successful bloggers understand that technology challenges will never fully go away. Technology is both a friend and an enemy. Successful bloggers embrace the mindset of resilience and see it as a core tool in their toolbox. Without the mindset of resilience, our focus is solely placed on our own lack of competence. Lack of competence leads to doubt, which leads to analysis paralysis. For too many years, analysis paralysis was the ruler of my life. Each and every day it sat on my shoulder offering me all the reasons why I should leave my proverbial boat tied to the shore. It squashed every new idea, project, goal or thought. It encouraged me "to play it safe." Finally, one day, I'd had enough.

Why Deciding to Fail Might Be Your Next Best Move

"I'm ready to just go fail at something!" That's what I told my coworker one night back in 2002 while standing in the parking lot after work. I didn't realize it at the time, but looking back now, I can see that a mindset shift happened in me. *The pain of not going for my dreams was greater than the fear of trying and failing.*

Over the next few years, I went from someone feeling stuck to a man on a mission:

- I bought and sold an investment property that netted $12,000 in 90 days
- I used the real estate profit to join a startup executive search firm, which led to a six-figure income for several years (all on 100% commission with no salary)
- I started two successful blogs, which created a time-freeing business for me.

Until you get to that place of *ready to fail*, you will still be stuck in the resistance. Your thoughts will remind you of:

- The things you don't yet know that might be lurking around the corner
- All the reasons why you are not ready
- How other people are so much better than you
- Why you should just play it safe and stay where you are

Perfectionism is Just Resistance in Disguise

Perfectionism is really just resistance if...

1. It covers your underlying fear of rejection. Being honest with yourself is so crucial. No one likes being rejected. No one likes being a failure. Yet, it has been proven time and time again that most successful people have plenty of failures to speak of. Peter Drucker sums it up best: "Whenever you see a successful business, someone once made a courageous decision."

2. What you are trying to do is more about you than who you are trying to help. What is the best way to overcome the fear of public speaking? Make your focus the message and about helping other people. If the goal is about delivering something life-changing, you become more excited than afraid. We often give in to the resistance because our focus is on ourselves. The same can be applied to starting a business, blog, product, or services. Place your focus in the right area.

3. It convinces you that the comfort zone is in fact comfortable. Is the "comfort zone" really all that comfortable? I don't think so. It just might be the biggest myth that exists. Perfectionism will keep you in the comfort zone. Resistance wants you to believe your life is better stationary. We all know what happens to water when it is stationary for too long. Take a quick evaluation of your life today and consider the following questions:

- Do you find yourself enjoying the learning process more than taking action?
- Do you write down goals only to abandon them within a few weeks?
- Does the pain of potentially failing feel worse than the pain of not taking action?
- Does the fear of not being good enough dominate your thinking often?
- Are you more interested than you are committed?

I am not a doctor, but if you answered *yes* to the majority of the questions above, then I have a diagnosis for you. You have the Analysis Paralysis Syndrome. The reason I can be so confident in my diagnosis is that I have been there. I have given in to resistance. I have believed the lie of perfectionism. What ultimately helped me to move forward was a renewed mindset of resilience.

9 Ways to Become More Resilient and Move Forward Anyways

1. Decide that the simplest solution is always the best solution. This principle took me awhile to learn. We often make things more complicated than they need to be. Occam's Law states, *"The simplest solution is almost always the best solution."* I often have to remind myself of this truth in my blogging business. In 2010, I wanted to launch my first online course. I wanted to offer my customers the ability to create a login and password on their own. I spent weeks looking at membership plug-ins and complicated software solutions. I quickly became overwhelmed.

Finally, I reminded myself of the truth that the simplest solution is often the best solution. That day I decided I was just going to password-protect a single WordPress page with a single password. The password I chose was *student109*. Every single customer got the same password. They thought it was unique to them, but it wasn't. This doesn't mean that we can't improve things along the way. Just keep in mind that the simplest solution is often the best solution.

2. Place a high value on the speed of implementation. Rewire your brain for action. When you learn something new that aligns with your goals, just go for it. We often drag out the implementation of an idea longer than necessary. Not to throw another universal law at you, but I believe it to be true. Parkinson's Law states, "*Work expands to fill the time available for its completion.*" Oftentimes we make a project longer than what it needs to be.

3. Believe that clarity comes from movement. We often try to get to clarity while standing still. It just doesn't work that way. Clarity comes from movement. You must try, test, attempt, launch, prove and examine before you get to clarity. Clarity doesn't come from resting under the shade of the tree but while jogging uphill on the road to success.

4. Don't dream big and act small. It is easy to dream big, but hard to "act in a big way." When we act small, we serve no one. As Seth Godin so eloquently said, "If you're not making a difference, it's probably because you are afraid." Our action should rise up to meet our grand vision. Resilience is when you care more about measuring your activity than your results. *Does your current level of activity match your grand vision?*

5. Decide to fail at something. The pain of failure is a big enemy. It keeps us in analysis paralysis. The biggest question I often get is, "What if I blog for an entire year and nothing happens? I don't want to waste my time." Trust me; I understand where they are coming from. What we bloggers often forget is that we are creating an asset. Worst-case scenario is to go sell your site at Flippa.com. Pretty good downside if you ask me.

6. See perfection as your #1 enemy. Many bloggers want everything to be perfect. They do not want to face criticism. They want every duck in a row before they take a step and they often want a guarantee of success before they start. It just doesn't work that way. Taking massive action without a guarantee of results is where champions live. Decide today to make perfection your #1 enemy.

7. *Only focus on starting.* Remove the obstacles from your thinking and just focus on starting. Set a timer for thirty minutes and just go after that task, project, or goal with reckless abandonment. You might be surprised how far you get in just thirty minutes. Just focus on *starting*. Overcoming procrastination and building resilience can be as simple as just starting.

8. *Focus your efforts in 90-day increments.* I mentioned earlier that a blog is best built "brick by brick." So, the next question is, "What are your bricks?" I see bricks as 90-day projects. Take out a calendar and divide it into four sections. For me it is as follows: January-March, April-June, July-September, and October-December. My whiteboard hangs on the wall above my computer. I currently have five projects that I want to get done in the next 90 days. I'll explain how I set up 90-day goals later. For now, just know that when I sit down to work, I know exactly what it is I need to work on.

9. *Believe that everything is solvable.* Often what separates the successful from the unsuccessful is their perspective during challenging times. It's always amazing to me how things work out for those who just *believe* it's going to work out.

The Deep Belief That Everything is Solvable

If there's a single core trait amongst full-time bloggers, it's the belief that *everything is solvable!* That doesn't mean we don't get discouraged at times. What it does mean is we know there's a way—either over, through, or around every issue. Even as I'm typing these words, all of my blogs have been down for nearly 24 hours. I'm losing out on the opportunity to gain more followers and earn money. I'm completely shut down at the moment.

My hosting provider is working on a fix and I know a solution is coming. So what is it that allows me to focus on typing these words when my main source of income is completely off-grid? My deep belief that *everything is solvable*.

You'll need to make resilience your friend if you want to walk down the path of becoming a Pro Blogger.

Chapter Eight

"Obsessive consistency sends a signal to my mind to focus and deliver serious results." ~Stephen King

Success Trait #5

CONSISTENCY

The faith that showing up regularly will create momentum

When my son entered into the third grade, we placed a sand pail next to the garage door. We live in Florida where most school playgrounds have sand. Every afternoon when he arrived home after school, he made a stop at the sand pail. He took off his shoes and poured whatever sand was in his shoes into that sand pail. Sometimes it was a lot of sand and sometimes just a little bit of sand. To be honest, months went by and I didn't pay much attention to that sand pail. However, one morning it caught my eye. The sand pail was now almost full! That is the power of the compound effect over time.

Consistency is the underdog of human productivity. We frequently celebrate the fast starts, big wins, successful launches, and massive victories. But we often overlook the daily actions, choices, and habits that lead to success. Every successful blogger wrote in obscurity for many months, if not years, before their audience showed up. Whether we say it or not, many of us want momentum to show up without the hard work. It just doesn't work that way. On top of that we are too busy, overscheduled, and worn out.

Myth #5: "I'm too busy. I just don't have enough time."

Have you said those words before? I know I have. We wear it like a mantle we are proud to display. It makes us feel important and gives us what we think is a worthy excuse for why we haven't jumped all in. We say it as if that's what successful people say. Unfortunately, we are wrong. Successful people make the time to do what matters most.

Work for Yourself First

A few years ago, I was seeing some success in my online business but not at the level that would allow me to do it full-time. Life already felt super busy for me so I wasn't sure what to do to get to the next level. My answer was 5:00 a.m. It wasn't until I made the commitment to wake up early, avoid normal distractions, and work for myself first that I began to seize some momentum in my business. I know what many of you are thinking: "I'm not a morning person." Well, I lived with that excuse for awhile until I asked this question: "How's that working for you?" If you want different results, you have to do different things. Choosing to work for yourself first before you give the rest of the day to your employer or family responsibilities can be one of the smartest choices you'll ever make. Here are five reasons you should work for yourself first.

Willpower is in limited daily supply. I remind myself daily that I start each day with a fully charged battery of willpower. If I wait to work on my business later, the focus, concentration, and commitment just aren't there. It could be different for you, but I am guessing probably not. Be determined to do your most important stuff early in the morning. By doing my creative work first, I start my day energized. In contrast, most of us let other people's agendas start their day. If your day begins with checking voicemails, text messages, and e-mail, you are doing reactive work first. No wonder you live frustrated. No wonder you run out of energy once you finally have time to work on your passion. Instead, choose to work for yourself first.

Fewer distractions happen early in the morning. I've also found that my early morning work session was completely free of distractions. I'm talking about both external and internal distractions. No one is looking for me at 5:00 a.m. The phone is not ringing at 5:00 a.m. I'm free to work. While I have to watch myself, internal distractions are less at this time as well. I remind myself often that I didn't wake up at 5:00 a.m. to surf Facebook.

The snowball effect is in full force. Never underestimate the power of flow and momentum in your work. Carving out consistent time to work on your passion is far better than carving out a full day. I get way more done in five one- to two-hour early morning sessions than I do in a single five-hour block of time. Again, I think this has to do with willpower, but momentum comes from consistency.

Joy is an incredible alarm clock. I wish I would have coined this phrase, but it comes from Jon Acuff's book, *Start: Punch Fear in the Face, Escape Average, and Do Work That Matters.* In the book, Jon makes the point that joy will wake you up and keep you up. This is how non-morning people turn early morning work sessions into a regular habit. There is nothing more energizing than having something to look forward to when your feet first hit the floor. In fact, I'm typing these words at 5:00 a.m. because I'm excited about writing this book.

Being normal is not an option. If being normal is okay for you, then stay on the road to average. Average is hitting the snooze button several times, rolling out of bed grumpy, hopping in the car late, being surprised at rush-hour traffic, and enduring a job for the weekends. If that is what you want, do that. If not, choose instead to work for yourself first each day. The consistency of this practice is what will create momentum for you.

The Faith that Showing Up Regularly Will Create Momentum

Consistency is the faith that showing up regularly will create momentum. Every aspiring blogger wants momentum but they're not sure how to get it. Momentum sounds exciting, like a rush of adrenaline. In many ways, momentum *is* exciting. But what it takes to create momentum is often boring. I say it is boring because momentum is built from the little things we do each day. Being fit and in shape sounds exciting—waking up early to work out before work is not so exciting.

What gets you through the seemingly boring moments? It's the faith that showing up regularly will create momentum. When you do what needs to get done today, tomorrow takes care of itself. The challenge many aspiring bloggers have is they live too much into the future. If they can't see in their mind how it is all going to work out, then why take action today? Pro Bloggers think differently; they live in the present moment. They have the ability to focus on what needs to get done today. Like Brendon Burchard says in his book *The Motivation Manifesto*, successful people ask the question, *"How can I better connect with this moment so that I can master what the hour demands of me?"* When you answer that question correctly enough days in a row and take action, momentum becomes your friend.

How You Start Your Day Matters

Mornings can be hectic to say the least. Most of us battle the morning rush, which includes getting the kids off to school and getting ready for the day ourselves. If you desire to work for yourself, how you start your day matters more than anything else.

In fact, how the first few hours of your morning go is how the rest of your day goes. If you start lazy and unproductive, it will carry into the rest of your day. When you work for yourself, lazy workdays are not optional. You work on "event" time and not "clock" time. You don't get paid by the hour; you get paid by *results*. Work the system in your favor and you don't have to work till five o'clock every day. Work until your most important objectives are done.

If there's one discipline that has helped me build consistency into my business, it's how I start my day. Let me share with you a few steps that will enable you to focus and get your most important work done early.

1. Start each day by answering these two questions. I journal in Evernote every morning. It's part of my morning success routine. I have a few questions (journal prompts) I ask myself each morning. Two of the most powerful questions are as follows:

What would make today great? This question allows me to take a fresh look at my work each morning. What's on my existing to-do list might not be the same as what I really want to get done today. This is an important question to ask each morning.

What are my plans for today? Even though I have a written to-do list, I like to ask this question as well. Typically, I will write down no more than five or six items that I consider to be my focus for the day. Sometimes it comes out of what I wrote in relation to the first question and sometimes not. Either way, writing down a new "must-do" list each morning gets you re-engaged on what matters most for your day.

2. Select your top priority and complete it before doing anything else. From the list of five or six items, I then determine which one is the *most* important one on my list. I then start my workday with what I call a "focus" session. This is usually a 60-minute, uninterrupted work session. I learned an important truth from Gary Keller's book *The One Thing*, and it is this: "*Until I finish my ONE thing for the day, everything else is a distraction.*" If you want to build momentum in your business, you must set yourself up for success on a consistent basis.

Notice that I've said nothing about checking e-mail or social media. I have developed a personal policy that I can't check e-mail or social media until my one thing is done. Is it hard? Yes. Because we are often addicted to e-mail and social media. It is a dopamine rush for many of us. We compulsively check our e-mail because we are secretly hoping there's something exciting and new waiting for us. If this is true, why not use it to our advantage; make it a reward for getting your most important thing done first.

3. Take a break, check e-mail, and social media. Once your most important task is done, take a break. Get up and walk around for a few moments. Go on a walk in your neighborhood. You also now have permission to check in with the world via your e-mail and social media. I can't stress how important it is to wait on your e-mail. As Brendon Burchard has said in the past, "The e-mail inbox is a convenient organizing system for other people's agendas." Don't get me wrong; it is important—it's just not the *most* important part of your day. If you want to be more consistent in your blogging, you must set up a system that protects your most important priorities. By putting in a few personal policies, you can become a more consistent person even when working from home. Remember, how you start your day is often how the rest of your day will go. Let's start productive.

You now know the difference between how successful people think as opposed to unsuccessful. Write down the five mindsets on a sticky note and place it somewhere you will see them. How you think matters. From your thoughts flow your actions. Decide today you will live with passion, confidence, patience, resilience, and consistency. A big question many aspiring bloggers have is this: "Where should I spend my time so as not to waste time?" Turn the page and let's learn about the four keystone habits of all successful bloggers.

Chapter Nine

*"Creativity is a habit, and the best creativity is the result
of good work habits."*
~*Twyla Tharp*

The 4 Keystone Habits of Pro Bloggers

I've conducted over ten reader surveys since 2010. I always
include an important question: *"What is the biggest challenge you face
right now in your life, career or business?"* The top response every time
has to do with time management. We are simply overwhelmed
with options. We are drowning in opportunity and paralyzed into
making a decision. We simply don't know where we should be
spending our time.

Most aspiring bloggers quickly become inundated with all there
is to do. We sit down to work on our blog and we could honestly
go in one of a hundred directions. The process usually goes like
this: "Should I spend my time tweaking my blog theme, updating
my plug-ins, writing a new blog post, recording a new podcast,
or fixing the broken links on one of my Web pages? Wait—I've
been quiet on social media so maybe I should tweet something
out, post something on Facebook, pin a picture on Pinterest, or
put it on Instagram. Also, I am curious what my blog traffic has

been like so maybe I should jump into my Google Analytics account. That reminds me, I'm close to surpassing 100 e-mail subscribers so I should also log in and check my list size too." Meanwhile, an hour has gone by and the rest of our life is pulling us away from working on our blog.

Are you beginning to sense why we feel so overwhelmed? The only cure for this challenge is for you to decide to be great at *just a few things*—the rest can wait till later. Full-time bloggers have figured out how to be great at the few things that give them the most return.

The Hourglass Funnel

Pro Bloggers are relentless with their time. They are not perfect. Just like all of us, they fall prey to lazy, unproductive days. But more often than not, they spend what time they have wisely. In fact, I've observed and interviewed some of the best in the world, and I've found that they spend the majority of their time in four key areas. I call them the four keystone habits. The four keystone habits of successful bloggers can be summed up in this simple graph.

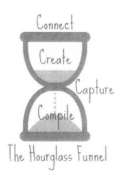

The Hourglass Funnel

The hourglass funnel illustrates for you how each of the four habits work together. All full-time bloggers spend the majority of their week in these four areas.

1. The middle of the funnel. We start in the middle because it's the most important part of the funnel. Without it, you have no business. Without it, success will always elude you and you'll wonder what you are missing. The middle of the funnel is the energy of your business. Ask any Pro Blogger and they'll tell you it is the most important thing in their business. It's building an e-mail list. We call this the *capture habit*. One Pro Blogger I know considers building an e-mail list to be so important that the only stat he tracks daily is: *"How many e-mail subscribers did I add today?"* Blog traffic isn't all that important to him as long as his daily subscription list is growing. In the pages ahead, you'll learn some of the favorite ways most Pro Bloggers build an e-mail list.

2. The top of the funnel. This is the hard work that many bloggers never do. To be successful at the top of the funnel, you'll have to give way beyond your comfort level. The top of the funnel requires you to roll up your sleeves and create value for others at no cost. Most of my mornings are spent in the *create habit*. Before you ever expect to receive income, you'll first need to gain influence and impact with your audience. Whether it's in the form of text, audio or video, you'll need to create massive value through taking massive action way before you ever receive massive income. The create habit is at the top of the funnel because all your free, high-value content is what's going to make your site attractive. Your free content is so attractive that people will want to get on your e-mail list. I'm going to share with you not only some practical ways to create content for your audience but also how to repurpose that same content so you can get your message out to the masses sooner.

3. The bottom of the funnel. This is often called "the back-end." The *compile habit* is where you'll spend your time packaging your knowledge and perspective into products and services. You're not really open for business until you have something to sell. Many bloggers want to put this off until they have lots of traffic and a large e-mail list. I'm going to share with you some shocking reasons as to why you shouldn't wait to monetize your blog. You'll also learn several ways you can earn money blogging your passion. It's also important to point out that the reason this is the bottom of the funnel is because it's much easier to sell to your e-mail subscribers who've received lots of free value from you already.

4. What pours into the top of the funnel. Once you have the top of the funnel (content that creates value), middle of the funnel (ways to capture e-mail addresses) and back of the funnel (ways to sell your knowledge and perspective), it's time to pour traffic into the top of the funnel. In the pages ahead, you'll learn how to do this through connecting with other influencers and going where your audience is already hanging out. We call this the

connect habit. Every successful Pro Blogger will tell you how much they value their relationships with other influencers. We'll be talking about the importance of partnerships and forming mastermind groups. Pro Bloggers don't see other influencers as competition. They highly value the opportunity to surround themselves with other passionate people who are heading in the same direction.

Spending a Week with a Full-time Blogger

What would it be like to sit next to a full-time blogger for a week —to be able to observe their habits and track where they spend their time? I bet you'd find the majority of their week is spent in four critical areas.

1. *Create*—Use text, audio or video to get your message out to the masses
2. *Capture*—The artful exchange of value for e-mail addresses
3. *Compile*—Package your knowledge and perspective into products and services
4. *Connect*—Build community with other passionate influencers

If you were to look at my weekly calendar, you'd find that the four keystone habits comprise 90-95% of my work schedule. Let's learn how to master each of these four habits!

Chapter Ten

"What makes for great art is the courage to speak and write and paint what you know and care about." ~*Audrey Flack*

Success Trait #6

CREATE

Use text, audio or video to get your message out of the masses

One of my favorite novels of all time is *A Christmas Carol* by Charles Dickens. Did you know that for years Charles Dickens wrote in obscurity? He spent three years writing for the *Evening Chronicle* for no payment. Eventually, much to the surprise of Dickens, he was approached by a young publisher who wanted to place his writings into a book. *The Pickwick Papers* made Charles Dickens the most popular author in the world.

Creating in Obscurity

Every successful author or blogger you follow once created their art in complete obscurity. Instead of giving up or being distracted by the latest shiny object, they just kept creating their art. If there is one distinguishing factor between the successful and the unsuccessful, it's that the successful keep creating their art.

Most of the e-mails I receive from bloggers have to do with how overwhelmed they feel about blogging. In the beginning, they were running off of pure enthusiasm. Just one nice comment would give them the fuel they needed for another week of blogging.

After awhile, most bloggers end up in the fuzzy middle—too far to turn back but not where they want to be. They often get lost in a sea of:

- Improving their blog design
- Gaining a presence on all social media outlets
- Finding ways to make money
- Facing technology challenges
- Trying the latest secret ninja traffic technique

My list could go on and on. There is no question many bloggers can get overwhelmed quickly. The quickest way out of the "fuzzy middle" is to eliminate the non-essential and focus on the essential. The first keystone habit is the "create" habit.

Create Value First

Before we dive deep into the best ways to create content for your audience, there's an important distinction to make. Your success as a blogger is not dependent on pure volume alone. The blogger with the most blog posts doesn't win. Neither does the blogger with the most ideas in his head. The blogger who wins is the one who creates the most value first.

Before you do anything else as a blogger, you need to create value first. Many bloggers resist this principle because they argue they will have nothing left to sell. Without creating value first, you will have no one *to* sell. You build an audience by creating value first. How then do we create this value?

The 3 Ways to Communicate Your Passion

Before we dive into the three ways to communicate your passion, it's important to note that you don't have to start by doing all three. I want to encourage you to pick one of the three, master it, and then add another one. Remember that it is more important that we remain consistent. If spreading yourself too thin threatens your consistency, you'll need to back down a bit.

1. Read What You Write (Text). One of my high-value activities each week is focused on writing blog posts. There has not been one week that's gone by since 2009 that I haven't published a new blog post. It's an absolute priority for me. I find that people still love to read and share helpful articles. Publishing new blog posts affords you the opportunity to pour into the lives of your audience. As you gain influence, you'll also gain credibility.

2. Hear What You Say (Audio). Your followers also want to hear what you have to say. Hearing your voice can bring about a personal connection that text cannot. They can feel the emotion, passion, and compassion behind what you have to say. This is why podcasts are so popular. Your followers can be influenced by you on their morning jog or daily commute.

3. Watch What You Do (Video). Many of your followers might learn best visually. Whether it is a screencast of your computer screen or a PowerPoint slide presentation, consider recording videos for your audience. You can share your videos on YouTube, Wistia, and Vimeo. You may even consider recording video of yourself. This is a great way to connect visually with your audience. They will feel better connected to you.

When it comes down to it, there are only three essential ways bloggers communicate their passion: text, audio, and video. Let's explore each of these areas a bit further.

<u>Text</u>—How to Create an Epic Blog P.O.S.T. Every Time

One of the struggles for many bloggers is the curse of the blinking cursor. It haunts them and they just struggle with getting started. The way out for me is to have a simple, repeatable process I follow for every blog post I write. To make it memorable, I've turned my process into a simple acronym. It gives me a template that is repeatable, while still being ideal for the end user. Each letter of the word *"post"* stands for an essential element of an effective blog post.

P—Purpose. Every blog post you write should have a single, defined purpose. For me, this is often the headline. I spend quite a bit of time crafting just the right headline. The headline is important because it is what people see first in search engines and social media. The right headline will also give you the boundaries you need to stay in as a writer.

O—Outline. At the end of the day, your blog post will either "educate" or "empower." If the goal of your post is to educate, then you need to answer the question: "How?" Picture your reader asking you, "How do I do that? Where do I start?" The outline of your posts will then be the steps your reader will need to take. I will often jot down the steps (or outline) before I write the blog post. If your goal is to empower, then you need to ask the question: "Why?" Picture your reader with their arms crossed. Your post will need to deliver the reasons that will persuade them to take action.

S—Scannable. An effective blog post is easy to scan. Most of your readers will scan a post before they decide to dive in deeper. By having subheads, short paragraphs, and concise sentences, you will make it easy for a reader to gain value. If your "nuggets of wisdom" are buried in the middle of a long paragraph, your reader will miss them.

T—Teaser question. A blog post should be the beginning of a conversation. By asking a great question at the end of the post, you'll encourage more engagement on your blog. I also like to use the teaser question on social media sites like Facebook and Twitter to get people talking as well.

<u>Audio</u>—How to Podcast Your Passion

In September 2012, I decided to take the plunge into podcasting. My topic was based on one of my blog names at the time, Simple Life Habits. I wanted to see if there was an audience in podcasting for my message of self-productivity, life habits, and time management.

What happened surprised me.

Within the first 90 days of podcasting, I had surpassed in listeners what took nearly two years to build in readers on my blog. That was even after having a few blog posts featured on Life Hacker. Needless to say, this got my attention. While you've probably heard much more about podcasting these days, many still think we are in the "wild west days" of podcasting. Consider a few of these stats on podcasting:

- According to Edison Research, one in six Americans have listened to a podcast within the past six months.

- The percentage of Americans who have ever listened to a podcast is 29%.
- 25% of podcast consumers plug their MP3 players or smartphones into their car audio system "nearly every day."

There is no question as to the popularity of podcasts. I personally think it is just going to grow from here. As I mentioned earlier, you need to master one before you add one. But if you are more natural behind the mic than trying to get your thoughts out in a blog post, let your podcast be the basis of where everything starts. For me personally, the written blog post is where it all starts and then everything else gets repurposed for the podcast or YouTube video. But I have other successful friends who love to start with the podcast. Regardless of where you start, you need to have a central hub you control—your own website. If you want to get started podcasting, here is the minimalist guide to getting started.

The Minimalist Guide to Starting a Podcast

Do a quick search on "podcasting setup" and you'll find many confusing diagrams. While there is no doubt some really cool equipment you can use in podcasting, you don't need to start with an expensive studio to launch a successful podcast. Here is a simple guide to follow:

Step 1. Choose your title and get your artwork. You may already know the title of your show, but if not, you want something memorable. Many podcasters choose either their personal name or blog name. However, it's also okay to go with a completely unique name if you'd like. For example, Michael Hyatt has a blog at MichaelHyatt.com, but his podcast is named This is Your Life. The artwork features his profile pic along with the name of his show. If you are not an artist, you can get your artwork done for your podcast for a low cost online. I know of several people who used a graphic artist at Fiverr.com and paid anywhere between $5-$15 for their artwork.

Step 2. Purchase an affordable, high-quality microphone. There are many great choices of podcasting microphones. You can quickly become overwhelmed by features and costs if you are not careful. If you are just getting started, all you need is a quality mic at an affordable price. Two of my favorites are the Blue Yeti USB Microphone and the Audio Technica Dynamic USB Microphone. Both of these microphones produce a high-quality audio for under $100.

Step 3. Record your podcast episode on your computer. Another reason I like both of the previous-mentioned microphones is they are USB and will plug in to almost any computer. There are podcast experts who don't advise recording your audio directly into your computer due to the fact that your recording software might crash in the middle of recording your podcast. While I am sure that is possible, I've been recording two weekly podcasts for three years and have yet to have that happen. If you are looking for recording software, you can use a free program called Audacity. I record all of my podcasts with a program called ScreenFlow. I can record both audio and video so it serves dual purposes for me.

Step 4. *Learn how to tag your MP3 file*. If you have never tagged an MP3 before, it may feel a bit technical. But once you walk through it one time, you'll be good to go moving forward. I once taught my virtual assistant how to tag an MP3 and she was able to pick it up after the first time even with no previous technical experience. Tagging an MP3 is what allows iTunes to extract the information they need such as the title of the podcast episode, the name of the author, the show notes, and the cover art. There are free software programs you can download to add this info to your MP3, or if you are familiar with iTunes you can right click on your MP3 and select "get info" to add all of the info there. An even simpler way is to use a service like BuzzSprout.com, which not only hosts your audio but allows you to upload any audio file. They will convert it into an MP3 for you and then tagging the file is as easy as filling out a quick form online.

Step 5. *Purchase a starter package for audio hosting*. Just like you've purchased Web hosting for your blog, you'll need to purchase audio hosting for your podcast. Even though it appears that your podcast episodes live on iTunes, the truth is all of the files are hosted on your own audio hosting account. The good news for those of you starting out is the monthly cost is either free or low cost. The audio hosting provider I recommend is BuzzSprout.com which I mentioned earlier. You can even start off with a free hosting account and upgrade later as you grow. Regardless of which provider you select, once you upload your MP3 file and hit *publish*, your show will appear in iTunes.

Step 6. Submit your new show on iTunes. Once you have completed all of the above steps, you'll need to submit your new podcast to iTunes for approval. This is a one-time action that needs to take place. The easiest way to do this is to go to the iTunes store and on the right sidebar you'll see a link called "Submit a Podcast." Walk through the steps and hit *submit*. It will take a few days to hear back from them, but then your podcast will be live.

Step 7. Get on a consistent publishing schedule. This is something I've had to learn the hard way. At times in the past, I've been guilty of being too ambitious with my time. This has caused me to be inconsistent with publishing my podcast. It's not a good thing when your listeners are e-mailing you asking if they are doing something wrong because they don't see any new podcast episodes. Decide whether your show will be daily, weekly, bi-weekly, or monthly and stick with it. Your listeners want to hear from you.

If you want to start a podcast, these are the minimalistic steps you'll need to take. If I had any other advice, it would be for you to not forget the purpose of your podcast. While you should be adding value, your main purpose should be to get them to subscribe. Subscribing to your podcast is good, but subscribing to your e-mail list is great. End each podcast with a call to action that leads them to signing up to your list.

<u>Video</u>—Spreading Your Message Through Video Blogging

Video is another great way to build an audience online. While you may not feel all that comfortable in front of the camera at first, you will get better with each video. I recently discovered some amazing statistics about YouTube. Did you know that:

- Over 60 hours of video is uploaded to YouTube every minute!
- YouTube receives over 4 billion views daily
- YouTube is the second largest search engine online

My daughter is twelve years old. She's growing up in a world much different than I did when I was her age. My days were spent adjusting the TV antenna so I could get a clear picture. My nights were spent trying to get the light attachment on my GameBoy to work so that I could keep playing Tetris in the dark. But things are different today. You can learn how to do anything on YouTube. Teenagers are becoming mega superstars by uploading videos they recorded in the comfort of their own homes. My daughter is self-taught in makeup, fashion, and cooking all from watching her favorite YouTube channels.

Today, the playing field is level. In days gone by, you had to either secure a television deal or "pay to play" for some air time through television commercials. We live in a different world. You can share your passion though video, build a business, and change lives. A video blog is often referred to as a vlog for short. Whether you want to post videos on a set schedule is up to you and the time you have available. Most bloggers I know have a YouTube channel as an outlet to post videos when it makes sense. It's another potential traffic source for them.

4 Types of Video to Create for YouTube

If you want to use video to spread your message, let me share with you four of my favorite types of video to create. The good news is you don't have to be in front of the camera if you don't want to. You can ease into the video creation process by using a few less intimidating options.

1. Create a simple PowerPoint presentation. Whether you want to use Keynote, PowerPoint, or Google Docs, you can create a basic template to use over and over again. You are not seen on the camera as the presentation is the only thing shown. Your voice will narrate the slides as you move through your presentation. You don't need to make this more difficult than it is. You can create great videos that are only two to five minutes long.

2. *Use an online whiteboard.* I love to doodle. I have three whiteboards in my home office that I am constantly using to write out ideas, thoughts, goals, and plans. Do a screen capture of you using an online whiteboard. While there are many to choose from, I like to use scriblink.com. I have probably used it to record over 100 videos. It is easy to use and I think it engages people as they are wanting to see what you are going to draw next. Again, you are not seen in this video. The recording is only grabbing your computer screen.

3. *Screen-capture your computer.* Performing a simple screen capture on your computer is another effective way to record video for your blog. This is ideal if you are teaching your audience how to do something online. It could be a video tutorial on how to use a specific software, a particular website, or how to do something on the computer. You are recording the video as if someone is peering over your shoulder and you are trying to teach them something.

4. *Record a video of yourself.* Also known as the "talking head" video, another great way to connect with your audience is to record video of yourself. This is one of the more popular methods on YouTube. That way people can get to know you and get a sense of your personality, and genuineness. Maybe you can stand in front of a whiteboard and explain a process to your audience? Use your creativity here.

Lastly, don't forget to embed your YouTube videos on your blog posts. Embed simply means that you can use some code that YouTube gives you to place your YouTube video right into your blog post. Doing this will benefit you in the following ways:

- *It engages the readers for a longer time on your page*. I have seen both my bounce rate drop and an increase in the length of the time that people stay on my site. I believe that these are factors that Google takes into account when ranking Web pages.
- *It endears the readers to you*. It's a simple way to build authority with your readers. They get to know you and your personality. They engage with you at a new level.
- *It adds tremendous value*. It is one thing to read about how to do something, but when someone shows you on video, it just makes more sense.
- *It increases the traffic to your blog*. Each short video you record can be uploaded to YouTube. Your video is able to pick up traffic on its own on YouTube. More and more people go to YouTube and do a search for their questions than ever before. If you paste a link to your blog post in the description box below your video on YouTube, you will be able to drive more traffic to your blog.

A Word on Repurposing Your Content

What's the best way to amplify and spread your message? The answer is to repurpose your content. You already have great content that can be leveraged to reach more people. For example, let's say you've been blogging for the past year and have over sixty blog posts. Many of those blog posts could make for great videos or podcasts.

What I have discovered is I have a different audience for each medium. Some of my audience enjoys reading but they do not listen to podcasts. Another segment of my audience only listens to podcasts and they do very little blog reading. Then there is an entirely different audience who loves to watch videos on YouTube. Repurposing your existing content can help you spread your message faster without having to come up with new content. You do not need to start off trying to do everything. Just remember that once you are ready to spread your message, you have existing content ready to go.

What's the Point of All of This Content?

You might be wondering what the point is of creating all of this content. After all, it's a lot of work, right? Well, first and foremost this is something you should *grow* into, not *go* into. Select either text, audio or video and only move into the next when you are ready. Repurposing your content will help you as much of the hard ideation of content has already been done for you. Regardless of what medium you use, the main point of all of this content is to create value and build trust—but more importantly, to get them on your e-mail list. As you will learn in the next chapter, your e-mail list is the life and energy of your business. Without it, you *have* no business.

Chapter Eleven

"The energy of your business is directly tied to the size of your e-mail list."
~Amy Porterfield

Success Trait #7

CAPTURE

The artful exchange of value for email addresses

If there is one unifying priority amongst all Pro Bloggers, it is the importance of building an e-mail list. If there is one major regret amongst all Pro Bloggers, it is not focusing on building an e-mail list sooner. In fact, *New York Times* Bestselling Author Michael Hyatt says, "Having an e-mail list is absolutely critical. It's my #1 strategic priority."

Building the "capture" habit into your blogging business is the single greatest skill you can develop. Remember, the reason it's at the center of our hourglass funnel is because it's the most important part of your business. We will be walking through a strategy for how you can begin to build that massive e-mail list in this chapter. Most Pro Bloggers believe that the size of their e-mail list is directly related to their income.

A few reasons as to why having an e-mail list is so valuable:

You can take it with you wherever you go. I had a mentor who taught me early on that as a blogger there are only two things you can take with you to the grave: *your reputation and your e-mail list.* In the last few years, many bloggers had jumped headlong into social media. They had tied their worth to the amount of "fans and followers" they had on social media outlets. All it took was for Facebook to make one decision to change their algorithms and many bloggers were at a sudden disadvantage. Instantly their engagement dropped overnight. Only ten percent or less of their fans were seeing their posts. Facebook had made the decision that you had to "pay to play" even though you earned those likes.

E-mail is still our main communication channel online. What is often the one thing you need in order to sign up for a new social media service? An e-mail address, of course. E-mail is not dead. It is more alive than ever. It is still the #1 communication channel for bloggers and will be for a long time to come.

E-mail is the most intimate form of communication. Adding value to thousands of people through their personal inbox is as intimate as it gets. Most people today are obsessive with checking their e-mail. It is absolutely vital to our professional and personal lives to do so. People can forget to check your blog for updates, but they won't forget to check their e-mail.

E-mail encourages feedback. If you are doing it right, sending an e-mail to your list should feel very personal. I often ask people to reply and answer a question for me. I once sent an e-mail to my list asking if I could meet them in person. I was surprised at the number of people who responded as if I had sent the e-mail only to them.

E-mail gives you the opportunity to create a buzz. When you are ready to launch a product or make an announcement about a new service you are offering, e-mail is the single best way to create a buzz. When I launched my first membership site, I gained 150 members in 90 days solely through e-mail. If you want an ideal place to facilitate promotion, it's in an e-mail inbox.

List-Building the S.M.A.R.T. Way

In Blogging Your Passion University, we teach our students a simple acronym that will help them to build a massive e-mail list. We use the word S.M.A.R.T. to make it easy to remember the different moving parts. Once you implement this system, your list will grow.

S—Some reason to subscribe. Many bloggers simply say, "Sign up for my newsletter." The problem with this call to action is people are more protective of their e-mail addresses than ever before. They are asking, "What's in it for me?" This is why you must give them some reason to subscribe. You do this through the artful exchange of value for e-mail addresses. Package together a "quick win" for your audience and they will gladly exchange their e-mail addresses.

A "quick win" resource might be:

- A simple yet valuable checklist
- A cheat sheet on how to use something that's a bit complex
- A simple project that can be completed in a few hours
- A toolbox that compiles several useful resources on one document

The most important thing to remember here is simpler is better. You want your e-mail incentive to be "quick to digest" and to produce a "quick win."

M—Multiple points of exposure. Once we have our e-mail incentive, we need to get the word out on our blog. Placing our call to action in just one location is not enough. Your average reader needs to see it multiple times before they will take action. This does not mean that we need to be annoying, just obvious. A few of my favorite places to display my e-mail incentive include:

- Top-right sidebar
- The About page
- After a blog post
- Featured box at the top of the page
- Notice bar at the very top of the page
- Strategic pop-ups

You don't have to do every single one of these to be effective. The point is to do more than just one. I think it is okay even to have different e-mail incentives as your visitors might have different tastes.

A—Autoresponder series setup. Want to put your communication on autopilot? That's what an auto responder series can do for you. First and foremost, you'll need a way to deliver your e-mail incentive you created. This should be in the very first e-mail you sent to them. From there, let me challenge you to create a few more "automatic" messages. The reason you want to do this is to build a relationship. Give more value to your new subscriber and they will be a lifelong fan. Don't just pitch them with a promotion. Instead, send them more value on your topic. In the beginning it can be as simple as pointing them to a valuable blog post you've written in the past. Just build the relationship. Shoot for adding at least five automatic e-mails over the first ten days.

R—Really specific calls to action. You need to have a clear call to action to get people to subscribe. They need to know what they are getting and why they should do it now. You may need to experiment with this but here are a few good phrases to start with:

- Grab your free e-book today
- Get instant access now
- Watch this training video instantly

- Download the PDF now

Start with a powerful action word and build a sense of urgency into your statement. You will get a higher percentage of opt-ins when you spend some time crafting a great headline.

T—*Traffic strategies that work*. The last part of our acronym is focused on getting eyeballs to our e-mail incentives. There are many methods and strategies for doing so. I'm going to share with you my top four ways to drive traffic to my e-mail incentives.

1. Free webinars. This has been my go-to strategy for a long time. If you have the heart of a teacher, you will love holding free training webinars. People love to learn, so getting people to sign up for a free webinar is not difficult. Think about it; if you only get 50 people to sign up for your free webinar, that's more than most bloggers get in a single month. I also love webinars because it builds the relationship. Your attendees can connect with you in a way no other medium can provide.

2. Targeted Facebook ads. While this does cost money, you can control it. You can spend as little as one dollar a day if you choose. Set a budget that feels comfortable with you and give it thirty days. Be sure that you target your ads and don't run them to the general audience. My favorite way of targeting ads is by choosing to display my ads to the fans of other Facebook pages.

For example, I created an Evernote course and sold it through a free webinar. I created a Facebook ad that only showed to those who liked Evernote's Facebook page. By doing so, I had many signs-up for the webinar because they were already interested in Evernote.

3. *Guest posts.* Where is your audience already hanging out? Go provide value there. One of the best ways is by writing guest posts. When you add value to others, they can't help but come and check out your blog. In some situations, you can place your e-mail incentive at the bottom of your guest post. I have a friend who used this strategy and added 500 e-mail addresses for a single guest post.

4. *Podcast interviews.* A super hot trend right now is podcast interviews. In some ways, this takes less time than writing guest posts. Basically, you find podcasters in your topic area who also interview guests. If you are featured as a guest on their show, listeners will come seek out your blog. We will be talking more about this in the chapter about connecting with influencers. My platform took a leap forward when I was featured on the Entrepreneur on Fire Podcast by John Lee Dumas. Once you get featured on a show like John's, you'll have plenty of interview requests come your way for a long time to come.

Building an e-mail list is the capture habit. It's the very center of everything you do. Getting people on your e-mail list is the art of capturing traffic. In fact, Pro Bloggers care more about how many people they are adding to their e-mail list every day than how many people visited their site. I know that might be hard for you to believe but it is true. I remember when my first blog first topped 80,000 unique visits to my site. I thought I had finally arrived. Only problem was my backwards thinking. My goal was to increase my AdSense earnings, so I removed my e-mail subscription form. I valued the $1.33 a click over building an e-mail list. Boy, was I wrong. Once I saw the error of my ways, my main focus switched to building an e-mail list first. That decision moved me from building a business that was like a deck of cards to a business built on a solid foundation.

"Having people on an e-mail list is great, but what am I going to sell to them?" I'm glad you asked! In the next chapter, we are going to lay out for you a 12-month plan you can start today to create five income buckets that will earn you income month after month. *Let's get started.*

Chapter Twelve

"Experts need to learn to package their information in a way that their customers can easily understand and implement." ~Brendon Burchard

Success Trait #8
COMPILE
Package your knowledge and perspective
into products and services

One of my favorite talks of all time is Dan Miller's *How to Make $150,000 This Year from Your Platform*. Dan opens up your eyes to the enormous possibility that exists for you to amplify a single message into multiple streams of income. It's what I've been doing since 2009 to build my own business. The best part is many of these products we can create today require little upfront costs and have incredible profit margins. Whenever I mentor someone and we get on the topic of earning money with your passion, I normally share the following list of ten ways to amplify one message.

10 Ways to Amplify One Message

You're not really open for business until you have something to sell on your site. While there are many different ways to monetize your platform, I'm going to share with you ten simple ways you can amplify any single message. Later, I will break this process down into a 12-month plan for you that I call the "Expert Product Wheel."

1. Kindle book. It's never been easier for you to write and publish a book. Amazon makes this process extremely easy. You don't have to wait for permission. You don't have to submit a book proposal and wait for acceptance. You simply write your passion and publish it for the world to see and buy.

2. Physical book. While there are certain advantages to going with a traditional publisher, you can self-publish a great-looking physical book. With a service like CreateSpace, you can convert your Amazon Kindle book into a physical book. Amazon will even sell your physical book for you without you having to carry the inventory yourself.

3. Online course. Compiling your knowledge into an online course is a smart strategy most bloggers are not taking advantage of today. After creating over ten online courses to date, it's my number one strategy for leveraged, recurring income. We will be going into more detail on this income stream later.

4. Membership site. When done correctly, a membership site can be a great source of recurring income. It can bring financial stability to your online business as customers pay you monthly. You'll need to think through a content creation strategy as most members of a membership site expect new content monthly. But once you have a realistic plan, you'll be glad you created a membership site.

5. Coaching/mentoring. If you are new to blogging or building a platform, opening up mentoring spots is incredibly easy. Your audience would love to be able to learn from you directly. You will need to keep in mind that you are trading time for dollars. To be effective with this income stream, you will need to charge what you're worth.

6. Audio book. It is also very easy today to take a book you've written and convert it into an audio book. With a service like Audiobook Creation Exchange (ACX) you can either hire a voice talent to read your audio book or you can do it yourself. Once completed, your audio book can be advertised for sale right next to your book on Amazon.

7. Physical products. With a service like Kunaki, you can easily convert any digital product into a physical product, like a CD or DVD. They will even drop-ship your product directly to your customer so you do not need to worry about carrying physical inventory yourself. It's as simple as uploading your artwork cover along with your audio or video file. You can then tie it into your website and allow your audience to purchase physical products from you.

8. Paid webinar series. While free webinars are an important strategy for me, when done right, paid webinars can be a great source of income as well. This allows you to receive up-front payment before you create the content. You'll then jump into an online teaching environment with your students and teach them. It's similar to hosting a live workshop but without the required travel.

9. Keynote speaker. Another great source of revenue is speaking before live audiences. As a blogger, you have plenty of helpful blog posts, podcasts, and webinars that can be easily converted into keynote talks. All you need to do to get started is to create a speaking page on your blog and have a way for event planners to reach out to you. If you go through the process of creating a framework that I'll share with you later, you'll have plenty of great talks that will lead to many ancillary sales.

10. Workshop leader. Why should I waste my effort planning in-person events if I can do most of this stuff online? That used to be my thinking for a long time, but my mind is changing. You will find that there will always be a segment of your audience who are "event goers." Instead of buying online courses or even paid webinars, they much more value learning from you in person, along with the added bonus of connecting with others and the chance to just get away.

Let me be clear. You don't have to do all ten of the above strategies to be successful. In fact, I've made the majority of my income in the past with just online courses. However, if you want to scale your business to reach more people, you'll need to repurpose your message into many different formats.

How to Create Your Expert Product Wheel in 12 Months

My goal is not to overwhelm you with options. The point of sharing with you the ten ways to amplify your message was simply to open your eyes to the enormous possibility we have in front of us. We will now focus our attention on a simple 12-month plan you can execute to scale your business quickly.

I call it the Expert Product Wheel. The reason, as you will see, is each step builds upon the last. The process can also generate an incredible amount of focus for you. As online entrepreneurs, we have no shortage of ideas or opportunities to pursue. By building your Expert Product Wheel, you will be scaling a single message into many revenue streams. In my mentoring programs, I often repeat the phrase "complete the cycle." It's my way of helping my clients to focus and follow through before jumping on to their next idea.

1. Create a framework that helps you teach your passion. If you spend time getting this right, all of the other steps become easy. Whether it is getting out of debt, eating more healthily, growing a speaking career or losing weight through exercise, your audience wants a roadmap. More than anything, they desire a trusted guide to take them through a proven roadmap. Creating a framework from your passion is one of the smartest projects you can undertake. A framework will help you:

- Organize your teaching into an easy-to-understand resource
- Scale your business by allowing others to teach your framework
- Write a book that explains your framework in depth
- Create online courses that not only deliver the "what" but also the "how"
- Gain followers so your audience can see the map of where you are going
- Design several keynote talks that can help build your business
- Give you a clear agenda to follow when hosting your own workshops

As you can see, building a framework is the essential first step. In fact, this book is an extension of one of the frameworks I have created. If you want an example of a framework, you can download the Blogging Success Pyramid at BloggingYourPassion.com.

Ideally, you'll want your framework to fit on one page if at all possible. Your framework does not need to contain everything.

It just needs to convey the big steps in an easy-to-understand format. If you are needing inspiration on how to graphically represent your ideas, do a Google image search on "framework" and you'll see many options. A few popular models include:

- Three concentric circles
- Pie charts divided into five or six parts
- Pyramid with blocks
- Baseball diamond with four main steps
- Staircase where each step builds on the next
- Ladder which represents different levels

You can even create something original like Stephen Covey did to explain his 7 habits of highly effective people. Going through this creative process will help you to simplify all your ideas into an easy-to-teach structure. *Timeframe: 30 days.*

2. Write a Kindle book manifesto that builds on the framework. Once you have your basic framework in place, it's now time to expand on it in a book format. While you can go the traditional publishing route, I'd encourage you to self-publish on Amazon Kindle. This will allow you to publish your work quickly and not be overly concerned with word count. Many Kindle books only average 10,000-15,000 words. In fact, most manifestos will average between 4,000-6,000 words.

The word count is up to you, but know there is no right or wrong answer here. What we want more than anything is a manual, guide, or manifesto that expands upon our original framework. Your book will provide the "what" in much greater detail. Since my framework includes fifteen traits, these naturally have become fifteen chapters in my book. The good news is that publishing on Amazon is free. In fact, you can sign up for an Amazon author account today.

If you want your Kindle book to also be available as a physical book, you'll want to reach a word count of closer to 30,000-50,000 words. This will allow your book to feel less like a pamphlet and more like a real book. By using a free service called CreateSpace, they will distribute your physical book for you when someone purchases it on Amazon. You can also purchase an inventory of your own books and have them for sale at speaking events. *Timeframe: 30-90 days.*

3. Create a coaching page on your blog to mentor others.
Another great reason to build a framework is to have a guide as you mentor others. I've been able to take different parts of my blogging framework and coach others based on where they are in their blogging journey. Putting together a coaching page on your blog should not take you very long to do. A few critical elements you will want to include would be:

- A welcome video explaining your coaching packages
- Testimonials from others who have been helped by your coaching

- Varying levels of ways to be mentored by you (example: one hour to three months)
- A way to accept payment (PayPal and credit card)

It's important to note that if you ever become overwhelmed by too many requests, you have the right to put "currently sold out" under your coaching options. I'd also recommend that you think through how many hours you have available for coaching each week. You are trading time for dollars and coaching should not be the only income-producing activity you do each week. A few benefits of adding coaching to your blog include:

- Staying current as to the real needs of your audience
- Testing your framework in real-life scenarios
- Seeing what's missing from your coaching that your audience needs

Make sure to advertise your mentoring page so people know about it. The first place I would advertise would be to place an ad in the sidebar of your blog. Another key place to advertise would be to add a link in the main navigation bar of your site. *Timeframe: 1-2 days.*

4. Create a speaking page on your blog with topics from the framework. Another fast way to create an income stream is to create a speaking page. What will your potential keynotes be about? You guessed it! Elements from your framework. I have at least five potential keynote topics from my single framework.

The beauty in this process is the way everything works together. If you deliver a killer keynote, people will want more. They will want to purchase your book, your online course, your upcoming workshop and even coaching with you. Are you beginning to see the power in this?

Just a quick note to those of you who have voices in your head at the moment. The voices might be saying, *"That sounds great but I'm not a great speaker, coach, or trainer."* If you are still battling the fear of not being good enough, I'd encourage you to go back a few chapters to where we discussed the importance of having the right mindset. You can do this. Just do the next thing.

What should you include on your speaking page? Here is a short list of items to include:

- Create content designed for event planners
- Record a short welcome video
- Share a bio of who you are
- List of your most requested topics
- Testimonials from previous speaking engagements
- Video clips of speaking engagements (if you have them)
- A call to action to get in touch with you

You can always add more later, but these are the essentials. Keep in mind you can always improve your speaking page later. The important thing is to get one live that displays the minimal amount of information you need to get started. *Timeframe: 1-2 days*

5. Create an online course or membership site. Nothing will scale your online business like launching an online course or membership site. While it will take some work for you to create your first online course, you'll have a way to get paid without being present. Nothing is more rewarding than waking up in the morning only to see you've made some sales while you were sleeping from a product you created a few months ago. This is when true leverage will begin to pour into your life.

Walking down this road will also free up more time to be more creative, which in turn affords you the opportunity to build even more leverage. Making room for your creative freedom is one of the most important things you can do as a blogger. I'm able to write this book because I have leverage. I have recurring income coming in from courses and membership sites I've created.

"But Jonathan, I don't have a big enough audience yet to launch a product!" Yes, you do. Maybe I was just a bit naive but I launched my first online course with less than 1,000 unique monthly visitors and less than 500 on my e-mail list. I had 15 sales on launch day and went on to sell that same course month after month. Nothing says you are officially open for business more than having your own product up for sale. Not only that, but nothing can build an audience like a product launch.

The 6-Step Blueprint to Teach Your Passion

Maybe creating an online course is a bit daunting for you. Seems like there are many moving parts and even technology elements you've yet to use. Let's break down the process into a simple 6-step blueprint. This is the same blueprint I've taught thousands of students in our Teach Your Passion course (You can watch a free video training series at: BloggingYourPassion.com/teach).

Step 1. The Idea Phase. If you are like most bloggers and entrepreneurs, you have no shortage of ideas. We often get paralyzed by this single question: "Which idea is the right idea for me to pursue first?" It's a valid question but it ought not to stop us from moving forward. My answer is usually decided by my audience. Even when I had a small e-mail list, I would survey my audience. In fact, before every course I've ever launched, I've sent out a short survey. It's super important that you understand what the needs and struggles of your audience are.

Before I launched Kindle Your Passion, which is an online course on how to write an Amazon Kindle book in 30 days, I surveyed my audience first. The first question I asked them was: "Have you thought about writing and publishing a Kindle book?" The choices were either "yes" or "no." When over 80% of them said yes, I knew this was a viable product to create.

Step 2. The Strategy Phase. Before we go and create an outline for our course, we need to decide how we will deliver our course. Will it be text, audio, video or a combination of all three? Will we sell the product before we create it or create it first? Here are a few options for you to consider:

- An online course (you create the entire course, and then sell it on your blog over and over again)
- A paid live webinar series (you get paid first, then create the content in a live webinar series)
- A get-paid-first online course (you sell the idea, launch with one lesson, and release the rest on a schedule)
- A fixed-term membership site (you offer a monthly payment plan for a fixed number of months)
- An ongoing membership site (you create monthly content and allow customers to stay as long as they want)

Step 3. The Outline Phase. Once you know the struggles your audience has and you have a strategy, it's time to put together a step-by-step solution. I strongly urge you to create an outline first before creating the content. Many first-time course creators fall into the trap of turning their course into an encyclopedia. They mistakenly think that covering every aspect of a topic means delivering more value. Your customers don't want an encyclopedia—they want a solution. They would rather learn a step-by-step process that leads them to a result. This is the power of what an outline can do for you.

Step 4. The Technical Phase. Let's be honest; we all have a love/hate relationship with technology. It allows us to accomplish some amazing things, but often fails us at the most inopportune times. Remember our chapter on resilience? This is where you need to preach to yourself that everything is solvable. The biggest advice I could offer you is to keep things simple. You can always improve it later.

Step 5. The Creation Phase. Let the fun begin! Follow your outline and begin to create that content. You will have to fight the resistance of being perfect. Don't try to be perfect. If you are creating audio or video, I think it's actually a good thing if you have some "ums" and "ahs." This will make you more genuine in the eyes of the audience. Of course, you don't want to come across as lacking in confidence, but the lesson here is don't try to be perfect. It's also helpful to write down a promise statement. What's the promise that your course is delivering? Let all of the content you create support the transformation you desire for your student.

Step 6. The Launch Phase. It's time to get the word out. Regardless the size of your audience, you need to create some buzz. By doing so your audience will share your product launch with other people. While whole books have been written on launching products online, let me share with you my favorite by far. My favorite way to create buzz about a new product is through webinars. When done correctly, you can convert on average 20 percent of your webinar attendees. There are three powerful reasons webinars work so well.

1. You have a live, captive audience interested in your topic.
2. They get a chance to learn from you for free.
3. They want to continue to learn from you so they buy.

This is why webinars are one of my most important strategies. If you are overwhelmed by the technology side of how to pull off a webinar, just start by hosting a Google hangout. They are easy to manage and easy for people to join.

As you can tell, I'm pretty passionate about creating online courses. They can provide you the influence, impact, freedom and income you are desiring. We live in an amazing time. There's never been a better time to teach our passion. *Timeframe: 90 days*

6. Host an in-person event or online summit. This last step of the Expert Product Wheel might be something you grow into over time, but it's worth mentioning here. I've seen people with smaller audiences pull off live events well. It does create anxiety for most bloggers because they are worried about not getting a good response. I certainly understand that fear. One way to overcome this is to start by hosting an online summit. The process is pretty simple and straightforward. Decide how many days your summit will last and how many speakers will present. Each speaker can present via a live Google Hangout with you as the moderator. You can make your event free or paid. Bloggers who offer their event for free see it as a list-building opportunity. They also sell the entire recordings after the event for a single price.

One of the great benefits of hosting an online summit is for pouring new potential customers into the top of your sales funnel. As they learn more about you, they will begin to purchase your books, courses, and coaching packages. *Timeframe: 90-120 days*

You now have a 12-month plan for completing the Expert Product Wheel. Let this be your focus but only one step at a time. Here is a breakdown again of your plan:

The Expert Product Wheel 12-Month Plan
1. Create a framework that helps you teach your passion (Timeframe: 30 days).
2. Write a Kindle book manifesto that builds on the framework (Timeframe: 30-90 days).
3. Create a coaching page on your blog to mentor others (Timeframe: 1-2 days).
4. Create a speaking page on your blog with topics from the framework (Timeframe: 1-2 days).
5. Create an online course or membership site (Timeframe: 90 days).
6. Host an in-person event or online summit (Timeframe: 90-120 days).

In a future chapter, I'll be sharing with you how to create a 12-month marketing calendar. This will help you to take this plan and begin scheduling deadlines for yourself. We have one more keystone habit that all Pro Bloggers do consistently: you must build community with other passionate influencers.

Alternative Ways to Earn Income through Blogging

What if you don't see yourself as speaker or an expert? Can you still earn a living through blogging or podcasting? Sure you can. While the above is a great plan for those of you who have a message you want to get out to the world, there isn't only one road to success. Here are some alternative ways you can earn money through blogging.

1. Affiliate income. You can earn a commission for recommending great products to your audience. For example, let's say you purchased a software for $100 that you absolutely love. Check to see if they have an affiliate program. Most affiliate programs will share 20-50% of the sale with you. Using our example, you could show your audience how you are using the software and earn $50 per sale. A great way to ramp up this income stream is to find recurring affiliate programs. Most of these are associated with services that offer monthly subscriptions. A recurring affiliate program might offer you $5 a month for as long as the person you referred remains a member.

I'm a part of a program similar to this that pays out $33 a month for each person I refer. As you can imagine, this type of income can build quickly.

2. Pay-per-click income. Wouldn't it be nice to get paid every time a visitor clicks on certain links on your site? Well, it is possible and it's called pay-per-click. One of the more popular pay-per-click programs is Google AdSense. It's free to sign up and they will pay you anywhere between 15 cents to $2.50 on average, depending on the competition of the ad.

It's also important to point out that Google AdSense is not the only player in town. Before I rebranded my career blog, I earned a monthly check from a job board on my site. I provided my audience with the ability to search job openings on my blog, and the affiliate partner paid me per click every time a user clicked on a job ad to read more. To be successful at pay-per-click you will need to have decent traffic coming to your blog, but it's still a low-maintenance way to gain an additional income stream.

3. Direct advertising. While direct blog advertising does still exist, there's a big movement in podcast advertisement right now. If you have a podcast or are thinking about launching a podcast, a potential revenue source is offering direct advertising on your podcast. The two most popular spots for ads are what are known as pre-roll and mid-roll. Pre-roll is a 15- to 30-second slot at the very beginning of the podcast. The mid-roll is a 15- to 60-

second ad in the middle of the podcast that might divide two segments of your show. More and more companies are seeing the power in podcast advertising. Probably one of the best examples for you to follow is John Lee Dumas over at EntrepreneurOnFire.com.

Before we close this chapter, I want to encourage you to keep your eyes wide open. New streams of online income are showing up all the time. When I first started blogging in 2009, I honestly only knew of three ways to earn income with my blog —Google AdSense, offering résumé makeovers, and career coaching. Just 24 months later, I had built 12 different income buckets for my blog. Successful bloggers keep their eyes wide open to new possibilities.

Now let's focus our efforts on building relationships and growing traffic.

Chapter Thirteen

"Successful people are always looking for opportunities to help others. Unsuccessful people are asking, 'What's in it for me?' "

~Brian Tracy

Success Trait #9

CONNECT

Build community with other passionate influencers

Total isolation. That's how I felt at the beginning of 2013. I had left a successful career as an executive search consultant two years earlier to pursue my passion for blogging full-time. I went from spending the majority of my workday connecting with people to isolation in my home office. At first, this was a welcomed break. Less people demanding of my time felt good. The ability to have creative freedom was just the jolt of inspiration I needed. Becoming increasingly isolated was not. Even though I had built several income streams in my online business, I knew I was hitting a potential plateau. Have you ever felt like you were hitting a potential plateau?

So, I did it. I chose just one word that would be my theme for the year: *Connection.*

I was determined that the theme of my year was going to be about connecting with others. I wanted to surround myself with other passionate people who were headed in the same direction. Study the best Pro Bloggers and you'll discover their desire to connect. The connect habit is fundamental to building a solid online business. If you recall, the connect habit is what pours into the top of the funnel. It could also be referred to as Web traffic. As you gain more followers, fans, and friends online, your traffic will naturally build as a result.

The 5 Sources of Blog Traffic

Before we dive into specific strategies for gaining traffic through connecting with others, let's back up and get the bigger picture of blog traffic. Google Analytics places all Web traffic into one of five buckets. By using their definitions, we can get a better idea of how people make it to our site.

1. Search Engine Traffic—This is traffic that comes from the search engines directly to your site. A few of the main search engine sites include Google, Yahoo, and Bing. If you've tried to do any research in the past on how to get more search engine traffic, you've probably left with your head spinning. There is no shortage of opinions on tactical plays for how to get more search engine traffic. I'll talk a bit more about this later in this chapter.

2. Direct Traffic—This is usually "top of the mind" awareness traffic. This is when someone directly types in your domain or in one form or another visits a page on your site directly. Having a memorable domain name can help to increase this kind of traffic.

3. Referral Traffic—This is one of the more powerful forms of traffic you can have. Referral traffic means that a user is clicking on a link to visit your site from somewhere else on the Web. This could be from guest posts, podcast interviews, or other bloggers mentioning you in their own content. Later in this chapter, we will discuss some specific strategies for gaining more referral traffic to your blog.

4. Social Traffic—Like it or not, we are increasingly becoming a more social Web. People will visit your blog and buy your products on the approval of others. While you don't have to be active in every social media channel online, you do want to make it easier for your fans to socially share your content.

5. E-mail List Traffic—I love that Google Analytics shares this data. This is blog traffic that is coming directly from an e-mail you sent out to your e-mail list. It means that they not only opened your e-mail, but they clicked on a link to come over to your blog. This is one of the main reasons "capturing" traffic is so important. By having people on your e-mail list, you are able to get them to visit your site over and over again. Without a list, they may only visit once, never to return.

If you are curious as to how you are doing in these five traffic areas, you can easily find out inside your Google Analytics account. Once logged in, look in the left sidebar and click on "acquisitions" and then "overview." This will display the five traffic sources mentioned above and how you are doing in each.

The Love/Hate Relationship with SEO Traffic

When I began my blogging journey back in 2009, SEO (search engine optimization) was all the rage. By following the advice of mentors, gaining traffic via sites like Google became the main focus of everything I did. I used to brag that 88% of my traffic came from the search engines. Today, I see it as a potential danger sign. Not that I want less of it, but it is an indicator light that I need to put more effort in the other four traffic sources that I mentioned earlier.

If you've followed SEO even from a distance, then you know that Google has a reputation for changing their search algorithm quite frequently. What works today may get you penalized tomorrow. I don't say that to scare you, but to prove why you don't want Google to be your only source of traffic. I do still think it is wise to practice the basics of SEO—just don't become obsessed with it. For most of you, the search engines may still represent your #1 source of blog traffic. While that is fine, decide to put more effort into your *connect traffic.*

The 3 Sources of Connect Traffic

The reason I'm bringing up traffic in our chapter about the *"connect habit"* is because I see blog traffic today as becoming much more social. It's a healthier form of traffic in many ways. As mentioned earlier, people buy on the approval of others. Your credibility can instantly increase when a fan or influencer mentions your work. The problem is most people approach this whole process the wrong way. They reach out to influencers asking for help instead of building the relationship first. I'll be sharing with you a better way to build relationships with influencers in the pages ahead.

I want you to see all connect traffic as falling into one of three buckets. While all three fall under "referral traffic" or "social traffic" as mentioned earlier, I think it will make much more sense for you if you see them in terms of followers, fans, and friends.

1. Followers—I define followers as those who follow you in some way on social media. They are probably not on your e-mail list just yet, but they do follow you from a distance. The key to reaching them is to provide value through their preferred social media channel. This becomes easy if you are regularly producing content in the form of text, audio or video.

Most aspiring bloggers don't do a great job of promoting their content. If you pay attention to the habits of successful bloggers, they are always creatively promoting their content on social media. They might take one blog post and creatively share that in several different ways over the course of a month. Here are a few ideas:

- The title of the blog post with a link
- A quote from the blog post with a link
- A fact from the blog post with a link
- An image from the blog post with a link
- An intriguing question with a link
- The intro paragraph of the blog post with a link

As you can see, your followers won't feel bombarded if you share value in a creative way. It's also important to note that you should be sharing other people's content as well. I also like to mix it up by sharing images and quotes. If you feel a bit overwhelmed by this process, I encourage you to take a look at CoSchedule.com. It's my tool of choice for both my editorial calendar and social media scheduler. They make it super easy to schedule both your old and new blog posts for social media sharing.

2. Fans—I define a fan as someone who is on your e-mail list. They like your work enough to follow you more closely. They either open your e-mails on a regular basis or they've purchased your products and services. They help bring you traffic by sharing your work with *their* social media followers. You need to make it easy for your fans to share your work with their audience. Here's two practical ways:

- *Add share buttons on your blog.* While this might seem obvious to you, every week I'm having a conversation with a blogger about adding social media share buttons to their blog. My favorite method is to have a scrolling share bar on the left side. As a reader scrolls down the share buttons stay in view on their screen on the left side. I've found that readers will share your content more if you make it easy for them. There are many WordPress plug-ins today that make this easy to add to your blog.

- *Pre-made tweetable quotes.* We all have one or two quotes in each blog post that really drive the message home. Make those easy for your fans to share on Twitter. A service called Click to Tweet makes this process easy. You can add a link inside your blog post at the end of a quote that says "tweet this." When a reader clicks the link, a Twitter window pops up with the quote already pre-populated. To make this process even easier, you can install a plug-in called Click to Tweet from TodayMade. You can also skyrocket your social media sharing by adding these tweetable quotes inside the e-mails that go out to your list.

3. Friends—When I first started my blogging journey, I saw other bloggers in my niche as competition. Did I ever have this backwards. Pro Bloggers don't view other bloggers in their niche as competition. They see them as allies. I wish someone would have told me this sooner. When I finally came to the light, I found that other more successful bloggers were way more generous than I would have guessed. I want to encourage you to build two types of friendships.

The Two Types of Friendships You'll Need

I don't believe that you can build a successful blog all by yourself. You need the influence and input of others. There are no self-made Pro Bloggers. Go ahead and ask each full-time blogger about their journey and they will bring up key relationships along the way. There's really two types of relationships you'll need.

Peers—A Circle of Wisdom

The first friendship you're going to need is a mastermind relationship. This is a small group of other like-minded people that you rub shoulders with regularly. As mentioned before, this journey can feel very isolated at times. The answer is to surround yourself with other passionate people heading in the same direction. You need a circle of wisdom.

One of my favorite examples of a mastermind group is the Inklings. This was a group of aspiring writers who would get together on a regular basis to debate out their writing ideas. In that group were two writers you'd recognize, C.S. Lewis (Creator of *The Chronicles of Narnia*) and J.R.R. Tolkien (Creator of *The Lord of the Rings*). As an inspiring writer, how awesome would that have been to sit in on those meetings? C.S. Lewis so strongly believed in the power of mastermind groups that he would later say, *"The only thing better than being wise oneself is to live in a circle of those who are."* This is why you need outside input to what you are doing as a blogger.

I have a virtual mastermind group that challenges me on a weekly basis. We meet via Google Hangouts every Thursday afternoon at 4:00. We spend an hour together in order to share our "highs" and "lows" for the week as well as those things we want to be held accountable for in our business. If you are struggling to get things done, maybe more than anything you need an accountability relationship that a mastermind group provides. If you want to learn more about launching a mastermind group, I've created an entire online course that teaches you the steps. You can get access by going to: JonathanMilligan.com/mastermind.

Mentors—A Circle of Influencers

The second type of friendship you're going to need is a mentoring friendship. While we immediately think about chasing the most successful influencers, I want to give you a different definition. A mentor is anyone who is doing better than you at a particular thing. This might mean connecting with an up-and-comer who has done something specific very well. In fact, forming friendships with bloggers before they are popular is an ideal situation to be in. They will bring you along in the process. That being said, you should still seek out major influencers in your niche. Just know there is a right and wrong way to go about this. The right way to reach out to a major influencer is often counterintuitive to most people.

Make Generosity Your Currency

Most people hate the word *networking*. It just doesn't feel right to them. It feels like a bunch of people trying to push their own agendas in order to get ahead in the world. Put in the mix important influencers and suddenly it feels more like junior high as you strategize what it's going to take to get a chance to sit at the cool table during lunch.

The good news is there's a different way. What if, instead of helping yourself, you decided to help others? Not only does it feel more genuine, but it's just way more fun too. There are things you know how to do that others do not. This is true with big influencers as well. Many of us mistakenly think that successful people have it all together. They don't. They face the same technology challenges and business challenges that we do. If you become a good listener, you will find the areas they need help in.

Just to be clear, the goal is not to keep score, but to freely help others. Your opportunity stream widens when you begin to help others. As Zig Ziglar always used to say, "You can have everything in life you want, if you'll just help enough other people get what they want." What are some practical ways we can connect with other influencers?

1. Share your audience with them. A great way to connect with an influencer is by promoting them to your audience. You might be thinking that your audience isn't big enough, but most influencers see it differently. They are grateful when other people share their message, product, or service with any size audience. A great way to personally connect with an influencer is to invite them to your podcast for an interview. What's great about this strategy is you'll have time to chat with them personally before and after the interview. If you don't have a podcast, interview them via video over Skype or a Google Hangout. You can then share it on your blog or on YouTube.

2. Help them overcome a challenge. If you listen closely, you'll discover the challenges that other influencers are facing. Sometimes it is as easy as reading through their past tweets on Twitter. I've seen many major influencers turn to social media when they are trying to solve a problem. Reaching out to them with answers is a great way to connect.

3. Introduce them to other influencers. Become a people connector whenever you can. You never know the type of long-term connection and friendship you might help make. They will always remember you as the person who brought them together. If you interview an influencer, as I mentioned earlier, simply ask them if they know [insert name of other influencer]. If the answer is a no, then connect the two of them via e-mail.

4. Buy their products and services. This is a terrific strategy most bloggers don't take advantage of. When you purchase a product or service from an influencer, you have a better chance of connecting. If their product has a forum, go in and serve their customers well by generously answering questions and you'll create a top-of-mind awareness in the mind of that influencer. You have brought value to their customer and made their product more valuable in the eyes of that customer. Also, purchasing products and services places you in a smaller community, which usually allows more personal interaction with the influencer.

The Fastest Way to Widen Your Opportunity Stream

The fastest way to widen your opportunity stream is to get in close proximity with others. This is why attending live workshops and conferences can be so powerful. Sure, it takes time, money and effort to attend conferences. But when done correctly, you'll be able to at the very least form an impression and at the very most form a bond. Either way, making the most of an event won't happen on its own. You are going to need to be intentional about a few things.

1. Have a business card to exchange. This was a huge mistake I made when attending my first conference. Everyone else was handing me a business card and I had nothing to give in return. Hard to form a bond when you don't give them a way to connect with you later. I determined not to make that mistake again. However, not just any business card will do.

You need to make sure your business card has these important elements.

- A picture of you—This is the biggest mistake people make. You want to be memorable, right?
- The brand of your blog—I've had people say, "Hey, I know who you are," just by seeing my brand logos on my card.
- Contact information—This should go without saying, but I want to take it a step further. As a blogger, you need to also have your social media links listed as well. Everyone has certain social media sites that are their favorites. This makes it easy for them to connect with you.

2. Determine to introduce yourself to others. Whether you consider yourself extroverted or introverted, you need to connect with others. If you are introverted, keep in mind that no one knows that. I believe that even introverts have the power to exhibit extroverted behaviors when they want. Also, once you meet a friend, ask them to introduce you to people they know but you have yet to meet.

3. Connect with people in a personal way. When you do meet someone in person, decide to be fully there. Don't look past them or appear uninterested. Lock in with them as if they are the only person in the room. Be sure to connect with them in a personal way. I've had people e-mail me days after the event thanking me for spending time with them and taking an interest in them.

You've just discovered the four keystone habits of Pro Bloggers. As mentioned earlier, 90-95% of my workweek is spent in these four areas. I know what you might be thinking: "But Jonathan, what if I'm doing all four habits but still feel like I can't get to the next level?" If you ask a full-time blogger, they'll tell you the answer is *systems.*

Chapter Fourteen

"Systems are the essential building blocks of every successful business."
~Ron Carroll

The 3 Systems Every Pro Blogger Needs

My favorite show on television is *The Profit* on MSNBC. It's a business-related reality show about struggling businesses in need of a turnaround. A successful businessman named Marcus Lemonis meets with struggling business owners to find out where they are failing. If he sees potential in the business, Marcus will offer working capital into the business in exchange for becoming a partner and having sole financial control. What's fascinating about the show is every business almost always has a great product and concept, and yet they are struggling.

Once the deal is made, Marcus gets all of the employees together to describe how they will operate, moving forward. Regardless of the type of business, he tells them that running a successful business really comes down to just three things: people, process, and product. Most of the time the product is not the problem, otherwise Marcus would have never invested his personal money to begin with. The reason they are struggling is mostly because of the process and sometimes the people.

What do you do if you feel like you are doing all the right things, but still can't seem to get to that next level? In the chapters ahead, you are going to learn the value of systems. For simplicity's sake, we will divide systems into three areas: processes, people, and plans.

Processes—Scale your business through documented checklists

Before you can even begin to outsource your work and get help, there's an important first step you need to take. That step is documenting your processes with checklists. The challenge for most of us is that we are already so busy this just feels like extra work. Our thoughts go something like this: "*I just want someone else to do all this other stuff for me so I can focus on where I work best.*" While that's a great mindset, we often jump over the first step. Because we don't take time to document our work first, we end up wasting more time by training and retraining those who work with us. They are stalled out because the checklist lives in our head. Even worse is when we have turnover and we have to start all over again with someone new. If your entire online business operates from your brain, you will always feel overwhelmed.

People—Leverage your time through other talented people

Once you've done the hard work of documenting your workflows and processes, you are now in the right place to get some help. When it comes to work, we all have green, yellow, and red activities. I like to describe each of them in the following ways:

- *Green work activities*—the things you can spend two to four hours doing and feel just as energized about them at the end
- *Yellow work activities*—the things you have competency in but don't enjoy doing and feel a bit drained afterwards
- *Red work activities*—the things in your work that are hard for you and completely drain you

The reason it's important to see our work this way is because each of us would label the colors differently. What might be a green activity for you might be a red for me. Your green activity is where your genius work lives. If the majority of your day is filled with red activities, not only are you drained but you are frustrated. Your red activities are someone else's green activities. Something that might take you an hour to complete will take someone else ten minutes and their finished work looks better. Successful bloggers have identified what their genius work is and they get help for the rest. We will talk more about creative ways to do this in the chapter about people.

Plans—Expand your brand through well-thought-out plans

Most aspiring bloggers operate with short-term thinking. Many Pro Bloggers operate with long-term thinking. They have a 12-month plan at all times. Having a long-term plan frees them up to focus on the short term. They want to get through the next book, product launch, or promotional plan because they have a schedule to keep. Beyond having a one-year marketing calendar, Pro Bloggers also have a few other plans that help to drive the business forward. We will go into more depth on each of these plans in the pages ahead.

As you can see, systems are important. Depending where you are on the blogging success pyramid will determine where you should place your focus. If you feel as if you've got a decent handle on the four keystone habits we covered earlier but want to grow to the next level, these next three chapters are vital for you. Let's get started.

Chapter Fifteen

"Top performers set their goals to improve behaviors and processes rather than outcomes." Joseph Grenny

Success Trait #10

PROCESSES

Scale your business through documented checklists

In the summer of 2013, I knew things needed to change. I had once again taken on too many responsibilities. I had aspirations for many things and new ideas seemed to be always knocking at my door. I knew I needed to put systems in place, but I hesitated. My last experience of hiring a virtual assistant felt like more work than it was worth (but that was my fault, which I'll explain later). Not knowing where to start, I began at the very beginning. Instead of jumping in and hiring help, I chose to be slower and more deliberate about what my needs were and where I needed help. Here are the five steps I took to regain my freedom and spend more time in my genius zone, while still scaling the business.

1. Evaluate Workload. When you are a busy blogger, the last thing you want to do is give yourself more work. However, we mistakenly think that if we just hire a VA, all our problems will magically go away. That's not how it works. So, I did what I'd resisted in the past: I decided to document my actual workday. I wanted to get clear on where my time was going. I had to make this easy or I wasn't going to follow through. I ended up using Evernote to document my work. On a Mac, the Evernote logo rests in your menu bar. Once you click on it, a handy Evernote note bubbles out. This allowed me to quickly and easily just jot down what I was doing. I did this for about a week.

Your Green, Yellow and Red Work Activities
As described earlier, you can divide all of your work into three colors. Doing so can provide amazing insight into which type of work excites you and which type of work drains you. As a refresher, here is how each of them is broken down:

- *Green work activities*—the things you can spend two to four hours doing and feel just as energized about them at the end
- *Yellow work activities*—the things you have competency in but don't enjoy doing and feel a bit drained afterwards
- *Red work activities*—the things in your work that are hard for you and they completely drain you

It's important to remember that green, yellow and red work activities are not the same for everyone. My red activities might be green activities for you and vice versa. Let me share with you some of mine so you can see how powerful this is in action. Organizing and creating content for me are green activities. I could spend four hours writing and feel just as energized at the end. A yellow activity for me would be fixing computer problems. I am capable of solving issues, but I don't enjoy it and definitely don't get energized by it. A red activity for me would be analyzing statistics and keeping up with spreadsheets. I see the importance of it, but it's not easy for me. I would much rather spend time on the creative side of things.

Back to the process. Once I had documented all the different types of work I was doing, it was time to evaluate it. I divided a whiteboard into three sections: what only I can do (green activities), what someone else can do for me (yellow and red activities), and what I needed to stop doing. Once you have documented where you are spending your time, evaluate your work so you can begin to make changes.

2. Eliminate Nonessentials. After everything made it onto the whiteboard, I began by deciding to quit the things under my "need to stop doing" list. This was hard at first, but it can't help but stare at you if it's on the whiteboard. I was surprised at how many things I was doing that just weren't all that important. Yet, these things were taking up a good portion of my week. What are the nonessentials in your online business? I was surprised at how many things I was doing that weren't important.

3. Engineer Processes. Remember the first virtual assistant I hired that was a disaster? Well, it ended up being my fault. I didn't take the time to create processes for her to follow. Since I had no checklist for how to do things, I was spending more time on training her two or three times on the same thing. This time, I decided to take all of the items under "what someone else can do for me" and create checklists for each.

I love checklists. If there is a repeatable process in my online business, then I want to document it, refine it, and use it. When it comes to creating my checklists, I use Evernote. It is a great tool for capturing all the repeatable tasks you are performing as a blogger. I love documenting processes in my business because:

- It is a great reminder for me on how I've done things in the past
- I have a best practices template to follow since I can improve this checklist along the way
- It offers me the opportunity to delegate tasks to other people who can help me

In some ways, our Blogging Your Passion University is a collection of best practices in the form of checklists for bloggers. You won't find much theory in our courses; what you will find are blog training videos that push you to action. Over a year ago when setting up my wife's blog, I actually watched my own tutorial videos from our university so I could remember the right ways to:

- Create a Facebook Fan page
- Make the necessary changes in the WordPress settings

- Create a Twitter profile and bio

It is difficult to remember everything all the time. This is why checklists can be such a great tool for your blogging journey. What are some of my specific checklists? Let me share with you some of the checklists I have in my Evernote account. I have checklists for:

- How to promote new blog posts on social media
- How to promote an upcoming webinar
- How to do the post-production of a podcast
- How to add a new podcast to iTunes
- How to prepare for a Skype video interview
- How to manage my Google+ Community group
- How to schedule tweets of my most popular blog posts
- How to structure the content of my webinars
- How to handle customer support issues

These are just a few of the checklists I am using in my online business. I would encourage you to begin creating checklists of all the things you are doing with your blog. Within a month or so, I had several checklists on how to run my blogging business. I also noticed something—it's easy to improve a process if it has been documented first. Once you have created a handful of checklists, you can then begin to use them in your regular workflow. Having checklists documented will help you in several ways:

- Which checklists do you need to have someone else do?

- Which checklists do you need to give some attention to and improve?

- Which checklists do you need to be reminded to do more often?

4. *Enlist Help*. Hiring a virtual assistant or crowdsourcing service provider became considerably easier as my documented processes now served as my job description. It's much easier to pass along a documented checklist to follow than you having to try to explain and even re-explain to your assistant how to do something. In the next chapter we will take an in-depth look at how you can enlist help without adding employees.

5. *Execute Core Gift*. Only when you do the first four steps above can you create enough space to get to creative freedom. Creative freedom is when you have time to do your best work. For me, it is about spending more time doing "the things only I can do." For example, only I can record a podcast episode. You are expecting to hear my voice. However, everything that needs to be done to the audio file after I'm done recording can be done by someone else.

Your business grows when you have the creative freedom to spend your time on your core gift.

Chapter Sixteen

"None of us is as smart as all of us." ~Ken Blanchard

Success Trait #11

PEOPLE

Leverage your time through other talented people

Have you discovered yet that you simply can't do all of this by yourself? It's true. There are no self-made Pro Bloggers. While from afar we admire the work of many full-time bloggers, we often don't see the team behind the scenes that help make this happen. I'm not suggesting that you need to go out and hire a team today in order to be successful. What I am suggesting is that you see your need for help as you grow. The good news is it has never been easier to get quality help at affordable prices. In this chapter, I'm going to share with you a few of my favorite resources for online entrepreneurs. They can be summed up into two categories: contractors and crowdsourcing.

1. Contractors—Working with Individuals

Contractors are individuals you work with who are not your employees. While some Pro Bloggers hire full-time employees to work with them, most do not. Most work with freelancers and contractors who work independently. Sometimes they are on retainer and sometimes they work on a project-by-project basis. The good news is you can find some super-talented people who specialize in a specific skill like videography or graphic design. The only bad news is they are only one person and they have plenty of other clients to tend to. You'll need to be okay with going at a slower pace in most cases.

When first starting the outsourcing process, most want to begin by hiring a virtual assistant. Since there is a lot of buzz online about virtual assistants, we mistakenly think that's all we need. Most of our thinking goes like this: "If only I can just find one person who can do it all for me, I'll be set." I remember early on in my blogging journey I thought my wife would be a perfect fit for this. Although she was busy managing the home, she wasn't working at the time so I thought I could just teach her how to do everything. Whether it's a spouse or a virtual assistant, you can't place all your hopes in one person.

If they decide to move on to something else one day, your world will fall apart. Depending on how long they have worked with you, you might not even have all of the things they did for you documented for the next person. You will also find yourself waiting on one person to get things done as they can only do one thing at a time. Just like you, they probably are not talented in everything either, which means you don't always get the quality of work you're hoping for. I think you are better off spreading your work among different places so you get more done in less time.

Elance—Some of my first hires came from elance.com. While there are several freelance sites like Elance out there, I prefer them for a few reasons. First, the customer support is great. They are located in the US and you are able to contact them via phone if you run into trouble. Other sites only offer e-mail support, which can be frustrating when you are in a bind.

99 Designs—If you need a logo or product image designed, then 99 Designs is a great choice. You can have a whole group of designers submit their idea to your project. This gives you the opportunity to see what several designers come up with instead of working with just one. The one-page framework I created for this book came from 99 Designs.

Fiverr—This is a great place to start if you are new to the idea of outsourcing. While you can up-level your service, most design projects cost just five dollars. You can also get a quick turnaround in most cases. When I needed a refreshed look for my Blogging Your Passion University logo, I worked with a graphic artist from Fiverr to get me the look I wanted.

2. Crowdsourcing—Working with Teams

There is a revolution happening in the way we outsource. Maybe you've noticed. The advantage goes to the solopreneur like you and me. With crowdsourcing, we can get quality work done quickly without having to hire full-time employees. One of the potential downsides to working with individual freelancers is that many of them have other clients.

Depending on their workload, you might be waiting a few days to get certain work done. The advantage of working with a service that offers crowdsourcing is there is almost always someone available to begin your task. It's like having a team at your disposal at all times. Someone is always ready to begin your task. While more and more of these service models are launching all the time, here's a few of my favorites for online business owners.

Fancy Hands (general admin work)—FancyHands.com is a team of US-based virtual assistants ready to receive your request. They can assist you in either personal or business matters. You pay one low monthly fee and in return you receive a certain number of tasks you can use them for. I've used them for various tasks such as:

- Research for quotes, stories and facts for blog posts, podcasts, and videos
- Light proofreading for blog posts
- Transcription of short audio or video clips
- Help with travel and lodging arrangements
- Calling to set up both personal and business appointments

- Managing my calendar
- Calling a service provider to wait on hold for me

It's a great service for those of us who feel pulled in a million directions. Before I jump into something, I often stop myself and consider whether or not it can be delegated to Fancy Hands. They also have a smartphone app which makes it easy to communicate with them when you are on the go.

WP Curve (WordPress and website help)—Before working with WPCurve.com , I either tried to solve my WordPress/website issues by searching on Google myself or hiring someone from Elance. With WP Curve, I have unlimited tasks each month for one fee. Their team of WordPress experts is not only talented, but they are spread out over the world. This means you can send them a task at night and it's often completed by the morning. When you start a subscription with them, they will even have their experts do an initial site review for you. The site review identifies potential areas of improvement on your site which can lead to better website performance and faster speed.

Undullify (graphic design work)—Images are important for most Pro Bloggers. With Pinterest, Instagram and other social media outlets, a great picture is worth a thousand words. You can even begin to develop a great brand through images. For example, Blogging Your Passion has a '50s retro look and feel. We did this on purpose. We wanted to distinguish ourselves from other experts in the online business advice space. Undullify allows you to pay one monthly fee and have unlimited graphic design work done for your blog. A few great ways to use this service as a blogger include:

- Images for your blog posts which also have headline text on them
- Cover art for Twitter, YouTube, Facebook, Google Plus and more
- Product images for a virtual product or course you are launching

Speechpad (transcription work)—From time to time you may need an audio or video file transcribed. You can use this transcription as closed captions for a YouTube video, show notes for a podcast or written text for a course or membership site. After cleaning it up a bit, I've even used transcriptions to create blog posts and Kindle books. Speechpad is a team-based transcription service. It's as easy as sharing the link to a YouTube video or uploading your MP3 file. I've always received great results from using this service.

As you can tell, there are many outsourcing choices for today's bloggers. If you want to do a bit more research on the service quality of any of these services I've mentioned, I'd encourage you to check out VirtualAssistantAssistant.com. It's a user-review-driven site that my good friend Nick Loper has put together. What makes it great is all of the ratings are driven by the users. This can help you to weed out the bad from the good.

What tasks should I outsource?

You should have the goal of outsourcing anything not in your genius zone. Your genius zone is the green light activities we described earlier. Another approach is to make a list of things "only you can do." Anything not on that list should at least be considered as an outsource opportunity.

For example, the things only I can do is write blog posts, record podcasts, and create videos. But all of the behind-the-scenes post-production is not something I have to do personally. Here's a running list of potential outsourcing opportunities for bloggers:

- Social media scheduling
- Post-production of a podcast
- Post-production of a blog post
- Post-production of a video
- E-mail monitoring
- Internet research
- Graphic design work
- WordPress and website help
- Transcription
- Proofing and editing
- Calendar management
- Managing finances

- Anything else on your documented checklists

As I've already said a few times, this isn't something you *go* into but *grow* into. Identify the biggest thing currently taking up the most time, and use one of the resources mentioned above to outsource it. Many of us hesitate to get started because we think we cannot afford it. A better question to ask is this: "How much more could I accomplish if I had help?"

Your focus needs to be on the four keystone habits. Specifically, more time spent in the *compile habit* means more revenue flowing into your online business. When you look at it that way, you can't afford *not* to outsource. Besides, as we have learned, there are several low-cost ways to outsource and still get high-quality work done.

Chapter Seventeen

"Productivity is never an accident. It is always the result of a commitment to excellence, intelligent planning, and focused effort." ~Paul J. Meyer

Success Trait #12

PLANS

Expand your brand through well thought out plans

For many years, I operated out of urgency with my blog. I'd come up with an idea, run with it, and then move on to the next thing. After watching the habits of more successful bloggers, I began to see they approached things slightly differently. It's not that they didn't have a sense of urgency; they just did a much better job with long-term planning. Because they had all their ideas plotted out on a calendar, they were able to fully focus on the next thing that needed to get done.

They operated from a place of organization and pace. These well-thought-out plans allowed them to make their products even better because they had time to brew in their own thoughts. They operated much more like a business—whereas I was operating my blog like a hobby. If you are ready to better organize your online business, it comes by way of well-thought-out plans. I recommend starting with three plans: *financial plans, marketing plans,* and *operational plans.*

Financial Plans

Assuming you want to blog full-time, how will you keep track of how you are doing? You need to have some financial plans and goals in place. I first started by tracking my income and expenses on a simple Google Docs spreadsheet I had created. At the end of each month, I would simply review the previous month to see where I had earned income.

This is an important habit because it shows you exactly what's working in your online business so you can do more of it. For example, I noticed one month that we were consistently earning several $100 affiliate commissions from each new sign-up for HostGator. HostGator is a monthly self-hosting service for bloggers. I immediately asked the question: "How can I make this better?"

The answer came in providing a simple, free blog setup service that took the pain out of new customers signing up. We began offering "free blog setups" for anyone who signed up for HostGator through us. This became a win/win/win scenario for all parties involved. We also saw our affiliate commissions double and even triple by doing so.

Tracking your sources of income in a spreadsheet can also keep you on top of where you need to get paid. This is especially true if you want to earn affiliate commissions as a source of your income. While most affiliates pay automatically at the beginning of every month, all of them are different; with some you have to wait to achieve a certain amount of commissions and then request payment. By taking a quick peek inside each of my affiliate accounts, I can see how I did and make sure I'm going to get paid.

My income tracking spreadsheet contains the following columns:

- *Payee*—This is the source of income I am tracking, whether it is my own product or an affiliate product. It can also be the link to the affiliate sign-in page, which makes it easy for me to check my earnings
- *Paid via*—This is important as every income stream can be different. Most pay by PayPal, some only do direct deposit to a checking account and others only pay by check.
- *Login/Password*—This makes it easy for you to keep track of all your login details since you are likely to end up with many different versions. Today, I use LastPass.com to keep track of all of them.
- *Month of the year*—Each month gets its own column on the spreadsheet. This will give you a great overview of how you are doing month to month. It's also a good

indicator that you need to investigate what's gone wrong if a consistent earner suddenly dries up.

- *Total at the bottom*—At the bottom of each monthly column, track your total. This will help you to see what you are earning in total each month. When I started tracking my revenue, I was only earning $500-$1000 a month at the time. However, this discipline helped me to get a big-picture view every single month.

Online Accounting Software for Bloggers

At some point, you may need to move to a more sophisticated system that offers better reporting. That was the case for me a few years ago. I needed to be able to run reports and drill down on certain data to see how I was doing. For example, one of my income streams is a membership site. I wanted to be able to instantly see what just my membership revenue was month to month.

I hesitate to recommend online accounting software because things are always changing rapidly. Instead, let me offer you the essentials you need as a Pro Blogger.

- *Automatic import of transactions*—Not all online accounting systems do this and some don't work very well. Most bloggers use PayPal as a way to get paid so you'll need a system that will automatically import your PayPal transactions along with your business bank account transactions.

- *Automatic categorizing of transactions*—It is also a big help if you can automatically assign certain repeatable transactions a category. This is helpful for reporting and tax purposes.
- *Simple reporting tools*—While you can get overly complex with financial reporting, you need simple reporting tools that can quickly give you the big-picture view of how you are doing in your business.
- *Ability to track quarterly estimated taxes*—The best-case scenario is to have a qualified CPA that you work with. However, a few online accounting tools will share with you an estimate of what you should pay in your quarterly taxes. Getting in the habit of doing so will help avoid nasty surprises at tax time.
- *Ability to publish a Schedule C worksheet*—This is the one document most CPAs will need from you in order to do your taxes. Also, categorizing your expenses correctly throughout the year can lower your tax burden.

Marketing Plans

Full of ideas without a plan. Does that describe you today? In the not-too-distant past, I was overwhelmed with opportunity. I had so many ideas I wanted to execute on and had no idea where I should spend my time. I was wrestling with:

- What should I work on first?
- Do I have the capacity to work on several ideas at once?

- If I have to choose, which of my ideas do I put on the shelf for later?
- How do I space out my ideas as to not overwhelm myself or my audience?

Then, one magical day in June, my wife said, "Sounds like you need a yearlong calendar so you can schedule all these ideas." That led me to creating a one-year marketing calendar. Putting together a marketing plan is the second of three plans you'll need, moving forward. This is a project I'd encourage every single blogger to tackle. A one-year marketing calendar will:

- Allow you to focus on one thing at a time
- Allow you to mentally forget a few ideas until the appointed time
- Help you to set a realistic plan of action (calendar doesn't lie)
- Give you a one-year track to run on
- Help you to say no to other opportunities that don't fit in your calendar
- Help you to say yes to opportunities by seeing spaces in your calendar

The 5-Step Plan to Launching a One-Year Marketing Calendar

Maybe you are convinced that you need this kind of clarity, but not sure where to start. Here is a 5-step plan you can implement over a weekend.

Step 1: Set up a 12-month visual calendar. Use your creativity here. The only requirement is to make it visual. When it is out of sight, it is out of mind. I simply went to CalendarLabs.com and printed off the next 12 months. From there, I found a space in my home office and I displayed all 12 months where I could view it every day.

Step 2: Color-code your brands, product launches, and events. The next step for me was to begin color-coding my ideas. This will help you to be able to visualize the different types of projects you have on your calendar. I purchased a few packs of self-stick markers so that I could move them around if needed. A few things you should assign a color might be:

- *Product launches*—I see each product launch as its own brand so for me I assign each their own color.
- *Group coaching*—A few times a year I do group coaching. This helps me to see what nights I have available to do them.
- *Membership site events*—Inside of Blogging Your Passion University we hold two live events each month. One is our Fast-Track Class and the other is a live Office Hours Session. I use a single color for anything related to our membership site.
- *Free webinars*—I enjoy hosting free monthly webinars. I'm a teacher at heart and love to share in these environments. I have a single color for all the free webinars on my calendar.

- *Book launches*—I'm working on two books at the moment and so I've set deadlines for when I'd like to release them in the next year.
- *Events/Keynotes*—I also have a single color dedicated to any events I'll be attending or keynotes I'll be delivering.

Step 3: Space out your ideas and amplify your focus. What do you want to complete first? Start placing your ideas on the calendar. Just choose a logical order; you can always adjust later. Also, be sure to create a buffer between ideas. We often underestimate how much work is involved in completing a project. Be willing to say no when things don't make sense. For example, my original idea was to host two free webinars each month. Once I began plotting ideas on the calendar, I realized that wasn't going to happen. I just didn't have enough free time on my calendar.

Step 4: Always stay six months ahead. This step is a tip to help you manage your calendar, moving forward. Don't wait until you complete your 12 months of projects to add to your calendar. I'd recommend you always stay six months ahead. In other words, once you are six months into your marketing calendar, begin planning the future six months in advance. This way you'll always have a 12-month calendar to work from.

Step 5. Set clear 90-day goals every quarter. Every 90 days I take at least one or two days to do a quarterly review. It's an opportunity for me to get a higher perspective on what's working and what's not in my online business.

Whether you are a full-time blogger or it's your side hustle, I want to introduce you to the power of setting 90-day goals. By imposing deadlines in my business every 90 days, I get more done. The deadlines for me are as follows: April 1st (Quarter 1), July 1st (Quarter 2), October 1st (Quarter 3) and January 1st (Quarter 4). I've been working this process for the past two years now and it's been nothing short of amazing for me.

Here's a few reasons why 90-day goals are so powerful:
- You gain incredible clarity as to what needs to be accomplished right now
- You are more motivated to work on your goals since you only have 90 days
- You get the opportunity to hit the restart button every 90 days

Sometimes we make this process more complicated than it needs to be. My process is pretty simple, but super effective. It provides me with the clarity, focus and motivation that I need to get my projects done.

How to Set 90-Day Blogging Goals

1. Select no more than five goals. I know you have a million ideas you want to get done in the next 90 days, but reality tells us that won't happen. You are better off selecting only a handful of goals. Keep in mind that these 90-day goals could be sub-goals of a bigger project. For example, if you want to write and publish a book this year, then a solid 90-day goal might be to create a book proposal. Use your 12-month marketing calendar as a guide to what you want to get done in the next 90 days.

2. Write your goals in a visible location. We all know that what's out of sight is out of mind. To overcome this, I place my goals on a whiteboard that hangs right above my desk in my home office. It hovers over me like a boss and draws me back in when I get distracted. Make your goals visible.

3. Start your goal with an action verb. We all know the power of words. Words alone can motivate us to action. There is a big difference between writing down "book proposal" and writing down "CREATE a book proposal for your new book by April 1st." The latter pushes me toward taking action. I also like to write my action verbs in ALL CAPS. It places much more emphasis on it for me. I use this same practice when writing down "to dos" in my task manager.

4. Make a short list of motivations for each project. This is a new practice for me and I give total credit to *Michael Hyatt's Best Year Ever Goal-Setting Course*. We need to be reminded often of the motivations behind why we want to accomplish the goals we have set. By writing down just a few motivations, you'll be encouraged to take action more often.

5. Start each day with a focus session to crush your goals. Writing down goals is great, but if you don't have a plan for taking action, nothing happens. When I sit down to work each morning, I first spend 60-90 minutes working on one of my 90-day goals. I do this before I check e-mail or social media. This one habit alone has propelled me to finish more projects than you can imagine.

Operational Plans

Your operational plans don't need to be more complicated than they need to be. I believe how you operate becomes your brand. A brand is more than just a cool logo. A brand is what others think about when they think of you. That comes out of what you value and how you operate. My operational plans come from reading the book *Work the System* by Sam Carpenter. Your operational plans can be divided into three sections: strategic objective, operating principles, and working procedures.

1. Your strategic objective. What's your big why? What are you ultimately trying to accomplish with your online business?

Writing down your strategic objective will give you much clarity. Don't be frustrated with the lack of clarity you might feel if you are just starting out. Some of this process will be revealed to you over time. To help prompt you with ideas, I've decided to share with you my strategic objective. I use the following information as internal documentation only. I don't share this anywhere on my blog. It's just for me and for those who work with me.

My Blogging Strategic Objective

As a blogger I endeavor to use my creativity and coaching to support and inspire others to reach their full potential for the glory of God. I want God's glory to be elevated in every word, project, program and blog that I create. By receiving hundreds of thousands of unique visits every month, I recognize the humble responsibility that I have to share the love of God with a lost and dying world.

Therefore, my main motivation for growing blogs goes beyond monetary value and moves into the realm of spiritual mission. I am committed to presenting God's truths in a non-offensive way in every blog that I represent online.

My fundamental strategy is to relentlessly serve others through teaching. Having the heart of a teacher and a desire to serve others is my core fundamental strategy.

My guiding documents are the Strategic Objective, Operating Principles, and the Working Procedures (inside Evernote).

My primary offering will be to create high-quality blog content in areas I am passionate about and to develop programs and services that can be scalable. By achieving scalability in my business, I am intentionally freeing up my time to do whatever God wants me to do without restrictions.

Competitive advantages include having a Christian worldview in every niche and passion where I have a presence online, developing relationships (lifelong customers) by going above and beyond what competitors may do, and avoiding hype in what we do and say (being authentic and real).

We will always be about growth. Not just when it comes to traffic, but in leading ourselves so that we can lead others. While we will operate according to our working procedures, we will grow with the times and change when change is needed.

We will remain playful by experimenting and testing new ideas. All the while, remaining above board in what we do and say (no spamming or black-hat techniques). We will keep close tabs on the results of our testing in order to measure whether or not something is useful. We will also endeavor to keep this playfulness in balance and not let learning interfere with taking the action necessary to grow our business.

2. *Your operating principles.* As mentioned before, your branding flows from what you believe (value) and how you want to operate (principles). As your business grows, you'll need to pass along these operating principles to those who work with you or your business will suffer an identity crisis. If you are just starting out, this may not be all that important, but as you grow, these become a necessity. If I decide to hire a contractor or freelancer long term, I share these principles with them.

The 10 Operating Principles for My Online Business

Here is a list of operating principles that will be the "rudder" of our online business. We will use the following principles as guidelines for our decision making. These principles flow out of what we believe and how we want to operate.

1. We are committed to producing original high-quality content that is both optimized for the search engines and useful for the end user.

2. The simplest solution is usually the best solution.

3. Constant and never-ending improvement is what will keep us competitive in the online world.

4. *Do it now* is our core philosophy. Speed of implementation must come out of our thirst for learning.

5. We choose to fight resistance daily and to "always be shipping."

6. The fear of not being good enough is never a good enough reason to not move forward.

7. Extraordinary results often require extraordinary effort.

8. We will always choose integrity over riches or making a quick buck.

9. The way that we treat each others matters as much as the things that we accomplish.

10. We will prioritize the resources that God has entrusted to us to their highest and best use.

Can you see how writing down some operating principles can protect your brand and help those who work with you to make the right decisions? Be sure not to get hung up on these principles. You may not get them exactly right on the first try. Just jot down some initial principles that are important to you.

3. Working procedures. For me, these are my checklists we worked on earlier. They are documented and they have specific steps to follow. Unlike our operating principles, our documented checklists are more fluid. They can change as we discover better ways to work and get things done.

Once you get systems in place, it's time to ramp up your business through leverage. Leverage has always been the ultimate wealth creator. However, it might surprise you as to the types of leverage Pro Bloggers desire the most.

Chapter Eighteen

"When we leverage, we aggregate and organize existing resources to achieve success."

~Richie Norton

The Two Best Ways to Leverage Your Business

After the release of the movie *Snow White*, it looked as if Walt Disney had finally reached the pinnacle of success. By May of 1939, *Snow White* would become the highest-grossing film in American film history, to the tune of $6.7 million in receipts. Yet, it would be well over a decade before his next smashing hit in the theaters. Why was that? What changed? What changed was the beginning of World War II. Instead of being bullheaded about producing more films, Disney chose to use the power of leverage through learning and listening. He created animated war films, designed to educate people about the war, which captured the nation at that time. This allowed his business to stay afloat until the war was over and he was able to place his focus again on producing feature-length films.

As you can tell, everything is changing at a rapid pace. To have a long career as a full-time blogger, you're going to need to see trends and be open for change in order to stay relevant. Any time I'm interviewed, there's one interesting question that almost always come up: "Where do you see all of this going in the next five to ten years?" It's a hard question to answer. Think about it. If you were to transport back 10 to 15 years, we were living in a day without iPhones and Facebook. Can you imagine a world today without those things?

Where all of this is going in the next five to ten years is hard to tell, but here's what I do know:

1. There will always be people who need help and I need to listen to them
2. There will always be others who are doing things better than me and I need to learn from them

If I always stay close to those two things, I'll be able to adjust with the times and find better ways to serve others. I call it the ultimate way to leverage your business.

The Two Best Ways to Leverage Your Business

When most of us think of leverage, we often think of earning money while we sleep, working our own hours and not trading time for dollars. While those are certainly benefits of leverage, there's an even more powerful type of leverage that all Pro Bloggers value. It comes in two forms.

Learning—The Ability to Unlearn and Sit at the Feet of Your Peers

It's easy to fall into the trap of believing that we know all of the right things. This is a pitfall of success if you are not careful. Some online entrepreneurs see success in one thing and they stick with it. They protect it like an only child. Only problem is they don't seek out advice and growth in other areas of their business. Then they wonder what happened when their business crumbles.

The most successful full-time bloggers understand the importance of never-ending growth. They have a unique ability to unlearn and sit at the feet of their peers. They are hungry to learn, and they recognize that they don't know it all. They have the ability to set aside their opinions about something in the past and take a new, fresh look at something old. Maybe they were once convinced that marketing on Facebook wasn't worth their time. Until they meet a peer who has an amazing approach to Facebook marketing. Instead of dismissing it, they open their eyes and listen as if it were the first time.

Listening—A Constant Awareness of the Goals, Passions, and Struggles of Your Audience

You cease to exist as an online business without customers, fans and followers. Successful bloggers can sense when they are becoming disconnected from their audience. This is one danger in scaling your business so large that you no longer have interactions with your audience. To stay relevant you have to stay in close proximity. What are their goals? What are their passions? What are their struggles? The more you understand the answers to these questions the better you'll be at serving your audience well.

As you'll learn in the pages ahead, staying in touch with your audience is absolutely essential. If serving others is your highest priority, then how can you serve them if you don't know their needs?

Chapter Nineteen

"When any real progress is made, we unlearn and learn anew what we thought we knew before." ~Henry David Thoreau

Success Trait #13

LEARNING

The ability to unlearn and sit at the feet of your peers

At age 13, a boy named Henry had a high curiosity for mechanics. So high in fact that he completely took apart the watch his father gave him. Henry then went on to meticulously observe and reassemble the watch back to working position. Henry became a lifelong learner of mechanics from that day forward. In fact, you probably know him by the name of Henry Ford. One of Henry's life principles was to always be learning. Later in life he was known for saying, *"Anyone who stops learning is old, whether at twenty or eighty. Anyone who keeps learning stays young. The greatest thing in life is to keep your mind young."*

How the ABL Principle Can Change Your Life

The ABL Principle is just a simple acronym I've created to stand for: *Always Be Learning.* If there is one thing you can be certain of in a world of uncertainty, it is this: *change is coming.* Those who are constantly upgrading their skills and expecting change survive. While others, who get too comfortable, get left behind.

4 Reasons Why You Should Become a Lifelong Learner

In the past 12 months, I have personally invested close to $8000 in courses and conferences. I intentionally choose to not rest in yesterday's successes in my blog or my business. As a result, I've become more resourceful, my business has tripled in growth and revenue, and I'm a more connected person. Here are at least 4 reasons why you should consider becoming a lifelong learner:

1. Fully develop your talents and abilities. Recently, someone asked me if I had ever written any blog posts on a particular topic. This caused me to dive deep into my archives. I pulled up a few old blog posts from a few years ago and I was embarrassed. The writing was bad and I wanted to just hit the delete button. While I am still not where I want to be as a writer, I can see how much I have grown over the years. You should be able to say the same about your core talents and abilities.

2. More easily adapt to change. Lifelong learners have an advantage in today's economy. They are able to make the adjustment where and when it needs to happen. When you are a lifelong learner, you can more easily:

- Switch careers when a particular industry dries up

- Make shifts in your business as demand changes
- Stay on top of your industry as an expert

3. Become the "go-to" person (resourceful person). One of the best ways to increase your influence is by being the most resourceful person you know. Be the biggest "giver" in any relationship. Help others without expecting anything in return. Go to forums in your niche and help others overcome challenges. Become a "go-to" person.

4. Meet people who share your interests. One of my favorite quotes comes from Charlie "Tremendous" Jones, who often said, "You will be the same person a year from now except for the books you read and the people you meet." While I still love reading books, I think there is a broader understanding of that statement. In today's high-tech culture, we can say, *"You'll be the same person a year from now, except for the things you learn and the people you meet."*

The Ability to Unlearn and Sit at the Feet of Your Peers

One of the great disciplines of successful bloggers is their ability to unlearn. As you become a more experienced blogger, you'll have to fight off the notion that you've already heard that, tried that, and dismissed it. You reach a dangerous place in your business when you think you have everything figured out. The most successful bloggers are learners first. Their desire for never-ending growth comes from a place of humility. They see their weaknesses just as much as they see their strengths. They make better connections with other bloggers because they are inquisitive. They love to ask questions and gain insights from others. They approach each relationship with a desire to learn from the other person.

If you want ultimate leverage in your business, you must cultivate the ability to unlearn and sit at the feet of your peers. It's the only way to innovative and stay with the times.

Become a Just-in-Time Learner

One of my core strengths is that I am a learner. I love to soak up new ideas, concepts, and thoughts and translate that into workable solutions for both my personal and professional life. Maybe you are like me and you are a "learner" too. Learning can feel like progress, and while this could be true to a point, nothing really happens until we apply those things we have learned. A few years ago, I was overwhelmed with all I needed to learn. The more I leaned into the idea of running an online business, the more I realized all the things I didn't know. This can be overwhelming for many of us. The answer for me was to become a just-in-time learner.

Just-in-time learning means you intentionally focus your learning on only those things you need to learn right now. Don't spend hours learning how to run a successful webinar if you are not willing to host a webinar in the next 90 days. Focus all of your learning time into a specific area that you're ready to take action on now.

Benefits of Just-in-Time Learning

Learn only what is necessary in the moment. This is probably the biggest benefit to learning this way. As mentioned before, only spend time learning something that you plan to implement right away. Cut out the desire to learn everything you can possibly learn from every kind of strategy that exists. For now, just do research on and learn something that you are going to take immediate action on.

Balance your learning-to-action ratio. If you spend one hour learning something online, find a way to spend one hour taking action on what you have learned. This will help you to keep your learning balanced and keep you moving forward. For example, if you want to learn how to produce videos and publish them on YouTube, then spend one hour learning the process and then one hour actually implementing what you learned. Keep track of how much time you are spending learning new things so you can balance things out. The reason it's so important for us to balance learning and doing is because learning by itself gives us a false sense of progress. Knowledge means nothing if you don't take action.

Accelerate your action ratio. Eventually, you will be able to spend twice as much time taking action as you do learning. A great ratio is more like 1:2 or even 1:3 if possible. For every hour you spend learning something, you spend three hours actually taking some action.

Becoming a lifelong learner will take you far in this business. Always be open to learning new things. Don't be afraid to try new things as well. Be a scientist. Scientists don't fail—they experiment.

Chapter Twenty

"If you listen, your audience will tell you what to create." ~Brian Clark

Success Trait #14

LISTENING

A constant awareness of the goals, passions, and struggles of your audience

Sam Walton, founder of Wal-Mart, highly valued what people had to say. He once flew into Mt. Pleasant, Texas, and gave his copilot some unusual instructions. He asked him to meet him at a location over one hundred miles away. He then hopped into a Wal-Mart truck the rest of the way so he could spend time questioning and listening to the driver. Sam understood the important principle of listening and gave it a high priority.

One of the hardest disciplines as you become more successful is to listen. You can begin to believe the lie that you've cracked the code and that you intimately understand your audience. The problem with that line of thinking is the fact that things change. The more distance you place between you and your audience the more misunderstanding can occur. You can begin to forget what it felt like when you were just starting out. You slowly become disconnected from the goals, passions and struggles of your audience.

Your blog is about them, not you. It seems so obvious and yet I find many bloggers who get this backward. I know there were times I had it wrong when I first started blogging. The tricky thing about blogging your passion is you can make your blog too much about you if you're not careful. I'm not saying you should never be personal or talk about your life experiences. Just remember what the end goal is for you. You are going about this blogging thing all wrong if your end goal is to:

- Make a lot of money
- Make a name for yourself
- Prove someone wrong about you
- Try to be successful in other people's eyes
- Live a comfortable life

Your end goal in blogging your passion ought to be to add value to as many lives as possible. In order to do this you must learn to be a good listener. The best bloggers have a 3-step process. Write. Listen. Adjust.

I love this quote: *If you listen, your audience will tell you what to create.* ~*Brian Clark*

If you're just writing and not listening, blogging can become weary. It feels more like forcing words on a page to just check the box instead of to change a life. While not every post can be epic enough to change the world, it ought to change *someone's* world. There is nothing more exciting than to answer a question, solve a problem, change a perspective, or offer hope to the discouraged.

But it all starts with listening.

Understanding Your Audience's GPS

Dennis McIntee often talks about the importance of understanding your audience's GPS. It's a simple acronym that stands for goals, passions, and struggles. You're a good listener when you're intimately well acquainted with the answers of these three questions.

What are their goals? Whether we've written them down somewhere or not, we all have goals. We have dreams, desires, aspirations and things we hope to accomplish. Do you know what those specific goals are for your audience? Listen for them in blog comments, social media posts, e-mails, forum discussions and reader surveys.

What are their passions? Have you ever seen someone light up in a conversation when you've discovered the thing they are passionate about? Whether it is about parenting, politics, snowboarding, surfing, camping, or being an entrepreneur, we are all highly motivated and energized about our passions. We gain an instant friend when someone is interested in our passions. What are the passions of your audience?

What are their struggles? Many of us feel alone in our struggles. Too many gurus only share their successes. They forget that their audience will connect with them at a deeper level if only they'd share their struggles too. Leading your tribe well begins by understanding their struggles. How can we recommend solutions unless we've walked a mile in their worn-out shoes first? Only through listening well can you begin to truly understand the struggles of your audience.

The Single Most Powerful Way to Listen to Your Audience

Successful bloggers understand the value of creating a continual feedback loop. Your content, products, and services should always be in the iteration phase in order to better serve the needs of your audience. One easy way to begin this feedback loop is using online surveys. I used a simple survey to create my very first online course back in 2009. By surveying my audience first, I had them tell me what they wanted in an online course about job searching.

Over the years, I have gone back to this strategy over and over again. Just the other day, a reader sent me an e-mail and asked, "I am creating a survey regarding my site and the changes we have made and plan to make. Any suggestions on how to phrase the questions to get good feedback?"

Getting feedback and insights is smart regardless of how small or large your audience might be. If you survey your audience correctly, you can use the feedback you receive to:

- Develop a content strategy or editorial calendar for your blog
- Create courses your audience will buy because you understand their pain points
- Understand the biggest challenge your audience has so you can connect with them on a deeper level

I want to share with you four easy steps that I shared with her. I encourage you to use this step-by-step system for yourself.

1. Set up an online survey. There are many great resources for doing this. To see the tools that I use, visit: BloggingYourPassion.com/recommended. You want to make it as easy as possible for your audience to participate. By using software designed for this, it makes getting feedback extremely easy.

2. Keep the survey as short as possible (3 to 5 questions). This is where many people go wrong with surveys. I would rather have fewer questions and higher participation. If you want a higher participation rate, keep your surveys under five questions max. Think about it: how many survey requests have you received only to abandon them when you saw they might be a few pages long? People are busy and you need to make it simple to get them to participate.

If you want some specific guidance in this area, here are what I believe to be the three most powerful survey questions you can ask your audience:

- What is the biggest struggle you currently have with
  _____?
- What types of topics do you enjoy reading about? (check all that apply)
- What would you most like to learn about in the next 12 months? (check all that apply)

With just three questions, I can fill my plate full of content ideas, products to create, and gain a better overall understanding of my audience in general.

3. Offer a gift card drawing for participation. If you want to really ramp up the number of responses you receive, then offer to give away a few gift cards for those who enter. Some bloggers don't like to do this because they are worried it might skew the results. While that might be true, I have found it to be worth the risk because most people will still answer the questions honestly. The bottom line is people like entering into drawings. A simple way to do this is to offer an Amazon gift card. You can send them their prize via e-mail so be sure to ask for your survey participants' e-mail addresses.

4. E-mail them, then e-mail them again. Be sure to remind your e-mail list about your survey. Also, consider sending additional e-mails to those who did not open your prior e-mail. You can do this inside your e-mail subscription service. You'll want to send additional e-mails because maybe they just did not see it the first time. You will also come across as less obnoxious if you only re-send the e-mail to those who did not open your first e-mail. You can also consider writing a post about your survey and pasting the survey link at the end of it. I've even created a sidebar graphic asking my audience to participate that way. Get creative and get your survey out there.

No matter how successful you become, decide today to never grow out of touch with your audience. Listening takes hard work, but it is required to remain relevant. Only when you deeply understand the goals, passions, and struggles of your audience can you begin to leverage the knowledge into value.

Chapter Twenty One

"Authority is always built on service and sacrifice." ~James C. Hunter

Success Trait #15

TRUST/AUTHORITY

The ultimate gift from a lifetime of serving others

What's the ultimate result we want from all of this hard work? For me it's not money, although I need money to live and reach my goals. It's not fame or popularity. I find more fulfillment in stewarding the gifts God has given me even if popularity never comes my way. The final success trait cannot be achieved as a goal. Instead, it's a result of doing everything else well. It's the ultimate gift from a lifetime of serving others—*trust and authority*.

You are rich when you've earned trust and authority with your audience. This only comes through years of serving others. The only way to earn trust and authority is through service and sacrifice. It's willingly offering your gifts to benefit others. I love the quote from James Hunter who said, "Authority is always built on service and sacrifice." While trust and authority cannot be achieved through effort, there are attributes that can assist us in building that trust and authority over time.

The heart of a teacher. The best bloggers are teachers at heart. They can't help but share what they've learned. It pours out of them because more than anything they want to see transformation in others. They desire this more than wealth. In fact, wealth comes to them naturally, as a byproduct of offering value and transformation first. Your audience can tell the difference. They know when someone is trying to sell to them. People don't want to be sold to; they want to be helped. Never try to sell anything before adding tremendous value first. I've been asked in the past what I do to stand out from the competition. I tell them my strategy is simple—*I focus on out-teaching the competition.*

The sacrifice of a servant. You are nothing without your audience. You need them more than they need you. You have no business without their support. It's a dangerous place when you see yourself as better than your audience. You cease to serve your audience when you think you're better. I've always tried my best to over-deliver in everything I've done. If someone purchases a 60-minute mentoring session, I go 70 minutes. If they e-mail asking for advice, I give them more information than they were expecting. I'm against the idea of using "no reply" e-mail newsletters or keeping your e-mail replies to just a few words. If I'm too busy for my audience, my priorities are in the wrong place. Is it always easy? No. Do you have to make tough choices at times? Yes. Just remember; you are a servant first, business owner second.

The love of a friend. Sometimes the best thing you can do is treat others as if they were your best friend. When you are in a conversation, be there *fully*. Make them feel as if they are the most important person in that moment. Whenever I have a chance to interact with others at an event or a conference, I remind myself of a simple acronym I developed. It's called P.I.E. Each letter represents something very important to me.

P-Present. We can tell when others are not fully present in our conversation. They are often looking past us, at their phones, or staring into space. Others can sense when you are not fully present with them. Choose instead to look into their eyes and make them feel important, because they are. I love the quote from Maya Angelou, which states, "I've learned that people will forget what you said, people will forget what you did, but people will never forget how you made them feel."

I- Interested. A true friend shows more interest in the other person. One of the best ways to show interest is by asking questions. I love to ask questions. You can learn a lot just by listening to others. They have unique experiences, perspectives, and advice. Who knows—you might learn something big just by listening.

E—Encouraging. We all have experienced toxic, negative people. They enjoy spreading their negativity as a twisty way to gain sympathy and affection from other people. The problem is the wake they leave behind them. They leave others discouraged and they are not sure why. I choose instead to be an encourager. I look for ways to say something positive and empowering. That's what good friends do. They notice the good in us and remind us often of it. Even when we don't see it or believe it ourselves. Determine to leave a word of encouragement to others. Every day before my kids go to school, I remind them to make it a great day for someone.

As you can see, trust and authority is not a goal to be had; it's a result from years of being a teacher, servant, and friend. A legacy is not built from a cool product or from the making of millions. Teaching, serving, and friendship is what builds a legacy. What kind of legacy are *you* building?

Chapter Twenty Two

Putting It All Together

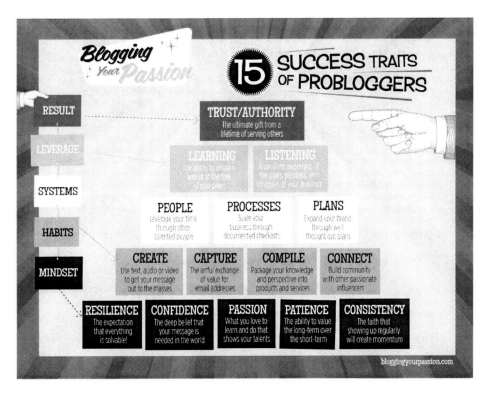

Congratulations! You're a champion. The fact that you have made it this far in the book says a lot about the type of person you are. You desire to make a difference with your life. You are not interested in living the status quo. You desire impact over security. You desire freedom over comfort. You desire legacy over apathy. You're the kind of person I love to be around.

We've covered a ton of material in this book, but I don't want to leave you without an action plan.

1. Print off the Blogging Success Pyramid. If you have not already done so, I strongly encourage you to print of the Blogging Success Pyramid. It will be a great reminder of the fundamentals you learned in this book. I even printed off the PDF and hung it on the wall above my desk. It helps me to remember where to place my focus and what I need to value. You can get your own copy by going to: BloggingYourPassion.com/book.

2. Check your mindset often. The first five success traits are all about our mindset. These mindset traits are important and even I review them on a regular basis. If my mind is filled with passion, confidence, patience, resilience, and consistency, I simply get more done. The reason you are procrastinating might be your mindset more than anything. Check it often.

3. Focus on the four keystone habits. When I feel overwhelmed, I go back to the fundamentals. Anything that doesn't fall under the four keystone habits gets pushed aside until I make significant progress there first. Like I mentioned earlier in the book, 90-95% of my workweek is spent in one of the four keystone habits. If you already live a busy life, just decide to do one thing in each of the four keystone habits weekly. This will build consistency and momentum in your online business more than anything else you could do.

4. *The roadmap is a journey, not a destination.* You might be tempted to try to do all fifteen habits at once. Unfortunately, it doesn't work that way. A successful blogging business is not built in a day. That being said, you now know the path. You have clarity as to what you need to do next. For the time being, decide which level of the pyramid you are on. Don't rush into building systems if you have yet to get a handle on the four keystone habits. In many respects, I'm still climbing the success pyramid myself. Sometimes it's necessary for me to back up a bit and get reacquainted with some of the fundamentals.

5. *Join Blogging Your Passion University*. A few times a year we open the doors to Blogging Your Passion University (BYPU). Our university is filled with thousands of passionate bloggers who want to walk the path with you. We have bloggers represented from every kind of niche you can imagine. Now that you have read the book, you can experience a deeper dive inside of BYPU. Each success trait is a module inside of the university. Each module contains five to seven blogging tutorial videos which are designed to help you build a successful blog step by step. We also hold regular live blogging fast-track classes along with open blog-coaching calls. To find out more go to http:// BloggingYourPassion.com/university.

Closing Thoughts

Walt Disney had a movie executive laugh out loud at his dream. Early on in his quest to bring cartoon animation to the movie theaters, Disney had what felt like an opportunity of a lifetime: through much hard work, he had negotiated an appointment with one of the largest movie industry executives at the time.

Walt's plan was to show him his seven-minute Mickey Mouse cartoon in hopes that he could secure a contract and have his short films shown in movie theaters across the United States. Walt was especially optimistic about this special meeting in the movie theater that day. He just knew that he had invented something revolutionary that everyone would want.

What happened next surprised him.

The movie executive didn't laugh at the cartoon; he laughed at Disney's dream. The executive went on to tell Walt all of the reasons why his dream would never work. "Kids are afraid of mice and moms don't love them all that much either. No one is going to pay to watch a silly mouse. This would never work," said the executive. With that the executive laughed and stormed out of the theater.

Has anyone ever laughed at your dream of building an online business? Has anyone ever given you the blank stare when you told them you wanted to blog, podcast or create videos? If so, it's not uncommon. Many people may not understand your dreams. If we are to have any hope of keeping the dream alive, we need to develop fortitude to move forward anyways.

Not everyone will understand your dream. Most of the greatest accomplishments in our lifetime once seemed impossible to many. Yet, there were a few who believed in the dream. They believed that a man could walk on the moon. They believed that you could hold a device in your hand and talk with anyone around the world. Don't allow one person's opinion to shut down your dream. Not everyone will understand your dream.

Believe in your dream even when others don't. What if Disney had given up on his dream that day? What if he had allowed one person's opinion to become his reality? There would be no Mickey Mouse and there would be no Disneyland or Walt Disney World. Getting negative feedback should not be a reason to pack it up and go home. You are going to need to believe in your dream even when others don't.

Focus on those waiting for your dream to become a reality. What then gets us through the valley when our dream takes a direct hit from others? Your dream survives when you place your focus on those waiting for your dream to become a reality. You have people waiting for you and your dream. They need your advice, perspective, solution and product. Whether you change someone's day or change someone's life, you need to make your dream a reality. We are waiting for you. There is a dream that only you can fulfill.

Surround yourself with other dream catchers. While it seems noble to charge ahead alone with your dream, the truth is you're going to need dream catchers along the way. These are people who catch the vision of what you are trying to do. For Walt Disney, he had his brother Roy. Roy's talent was in the numbers side of the business. He was in the background, helping to finance the dream while Walt focused on the creative side.

There were also employees of Walt who caught the vision. In the early days, he had animators work without pay because they believed in the dream so much. They worked nights and weekends in an effort to get the cartoon done. They were lost in their passions and Walt had inspired them. Eventually, all this hard work paid off for these animators—but in the early days they were there in total support of Walt's dream. How about you? Are there dream catchers in your life you've taken for granted? Take a moment today and send them an e-mail of thanks for being a part of your dream.

We need you to chase your dream. *It starts today.*

Thank You!

As a way of saying thanks for your purchase, we're offering two free gifts that are exclusive to our book and blog readers.

First up is the one-page roadmap that outlines the entire book. This is a beautiful color PDF you can print off and hang next to you as you build your online blogging business. It reinforces the 15 success traits you learned about in this book.

Next is a free video training series I have created for you. If you want to dive deeper into what it takes to go *from a passionate idea to a profitable online business*, then you'll want to grab this free video training series!

Grab the "15 Success Traits" Bonus Package

http://BloggingYourPassion.com/book

ABOUT THE AUTHOR

Jonathan Milligan is an author, blogger, speaker and business coach. He has spent the last decade counseling, guiding, and directing others on how to pursue meaningful work. Since 2009, Jonathan has been building a portable, lifestyle business through blogging. Today, he teaches others the roadmap to doing the same.

His two primary blogs are:

JonathanMilligan.com
BloggingYourPassion.com

Jonathan is also active in his local church, serving as a Deacon and leader of the hospitality ministry. He resides in Jacksonville, Florida with his wife and two kids.

CPSIA information can be obtained at www.ICGtesting.com
Printed in the USA
LVOW06s1643150915

454264LV00006B/1059/P